CLASSIC

# ARTS & CRAFTS FURNITURE

YOU CAN BUILD

# CLASSIC
# ARTS & CRAFTS
# FURNITURE
## YOU CAN BUILD

## ANDY SCHULTZ

**POPULAR WOODWORKING BOOKS**
CINCINNATI, OHIO
www.popularwoodworking.com

## METRIC CONVERSION CHART

| TO CONVERT | TO | MULTIPLY BY |
| --- | --- | --- |
| Inches | Centimeters | 2.54 |
| Centimeters | Inches | 0.4 |

**Classic Arts and Crafts Furniture You Can Build.** Copyright © 1999 by Andy Schultz. Manufactured in the United States. All rights reserved. No part of this book may be reproduced in any form or by any electronic or mechanical means including information storage and retrieval systems without permission in writing from the publisher, except by a reviewer, who may quote brief passages in a review. Published by Popular Woodworking Books, an imprint of F&W Publications, Inc., 1507 Dana Avenue, Cincinnati, Ohio 45207. (800) 289-0963. First edition.

Other fine Popular Woodworking Books are available from your local bookstore or direct from the publisher. Visit our Web site at www.popularwoodworking.com for information on more resources for woodworkers.

03   02   01   00   99     5   4   3   2   1

**Library of Congress Cataloging-in-Publication Data**

Schultz, Andy.
    Classic arts & crafts furniture you can build / by Andy Schultz.
        p.     cm.
    Includes index.
    ISBN 1-55870-490-6 (alk. paper)
    1. Furniture making—Amateurs' manuals. 2. Furniture, Mission—United States—Amateurs' manuals. 3. Arts and crafts movement—United States—Amateurs' manuals. I. Title.
TT195.S365   1999
684.1'04—dc21
                                                                                                                    99-10931
                                                                                                                    CIP

Editor: Bruce Stoker
Production editor: Christine Doyle and Jeff Crump
Production coordinator: John Peavler
Cover designed by Clare Finney
Interior designed by Brian Roeth
Cover photography by Paul Brokering

The photo of the armchair found in the Gamble House in Pasadena, CA on page 19 is published with permission of the photographer, Alex Vertikoff, PO Box 2079, Tijeras, NM 87059.

The photo of the sideboard found in the Thorsen House in Pasadena, CA on page 19 is published with permission of the photographer, Tim Street-Porter, 2074 Watsonia Terrace, Los Angeles, CA 90068.

## ❖ ACKNOWLEDGMENTS

*Many thanks to the following people:*

My editor, Bruce Stoker

My publisher, Popular Woodworking Books, represented by R. Adam Blake

My father, Lumir Schultz

My wife, Mary Sutton

My kids, Andrew and Nichole

My ever-supporting in-laws, Jack and Lorraine Sutton

My friends, Joe and Dan at Old Mill Woodworking

My friends, Buck, Gary and Bob at Hardwood Heaven

My upholsterer, Vickie Little

And finally, a special thanks to all who work wood. You are the best people in the world, builders and makers all. May your chisels be keen, your glue bottles full and may your woodstacks overfloweth.

## ❖ ABOUT THE AUTHOR

Andy Schultz is a former Taunton book editor, experienced woodworker, writer, teacher and photographer. He is the author of *Build Your Own Entertainment Centers* (Popular Woodworking Books) and many articles for woodworking magazines.

These registered patent trademarks of Gustav Stickley's Craftsman Farms indicate that not only is each piece of furniture an original work, but each piece represents Stickley's personal best.

# ALS IK KAN

—Slogan of Craftsman Farms craftsmen,
"The best I can."

# THE DINING ROOM

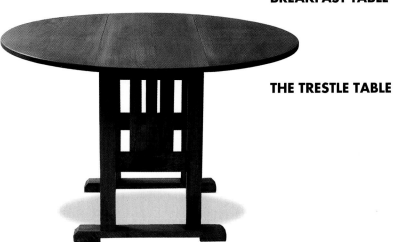

# THE BEDROOM

# THE DEN

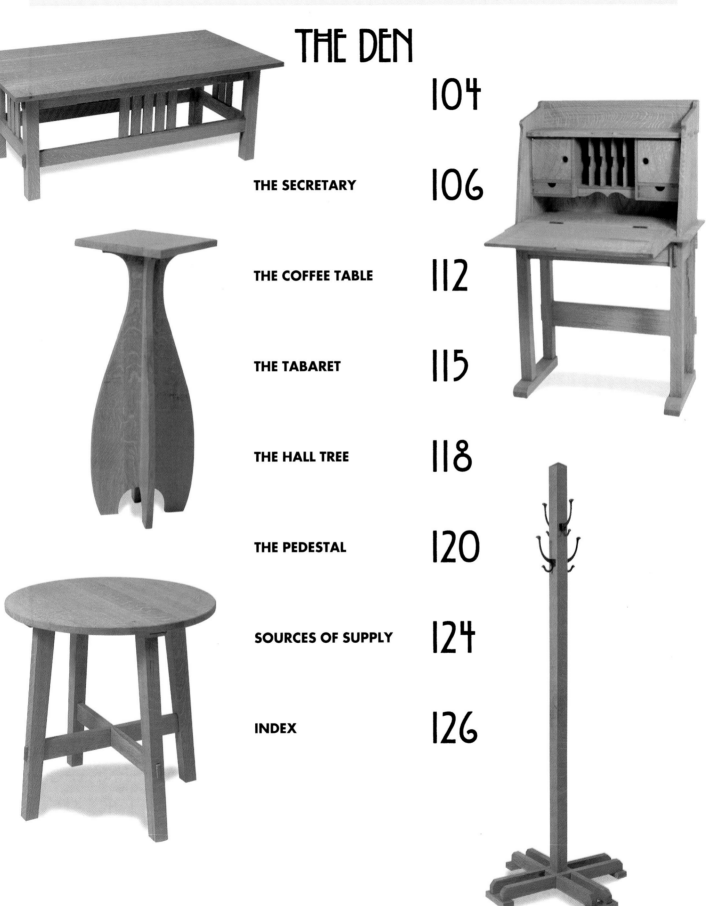

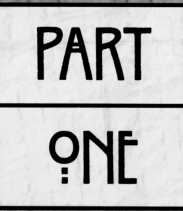

# PART

# ONE

Of all the causes supported by the adherents of the Arts and Crafts movement, none is so much at the center of it all, or through it all, as the concept of living the good life. Whether through social reform or through the return to simple pleasures or to simple designs in furniture and such, the proponents of the movement, in its various forms, were dedicated to making life more enjoyable.

"THE ROOT OF ALL REFORM LIES
IN THE INDIVIDUAL AND THAT THE
LIFE OF THE INDIVIDUAL IS SHAPED
MAINLY BY HOME SURROUNDINGS."

—WILLIAM MORRIS

# A BRIEF HISTORY OF ARTS & CRAFTS STYLE FURNITURE

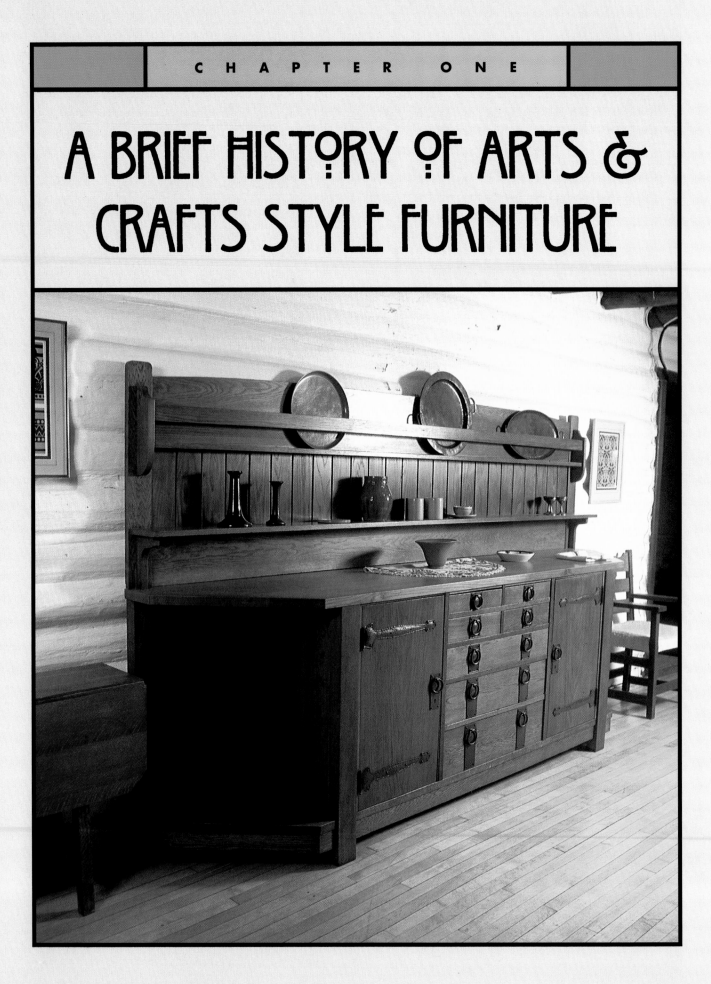

## JOHN RUSKIN AND WILLIAM MORRIS

The Arts and Crafts movement sprang from a midcentury rejection of shoddy manufactured goods in nineteenth-century England. You will no doubt recall the Victorian kitsch and the rococo zeal for cramming every inch of one's home with bric-a-brac and ornamentation. Two English gentlemen, John Ruskin and William Morris, began a crusade to rescue the workers from the arid, semiskilled monotony of the factory and guide them into an enlightened return to the craft ideals of medieval England. They wanted the material goods of their world to be honest and direct, and they wanted the craftsmen who created these goods to be intimately involved in both the design and manufacture of them. Many of the ills of the industrialized world came, they believed, from this disconnection between the appearance and function of the product. The joy of the craftsmen they saw reflected in Gothic architecture and furniture, in medieval tapestries and in illuminated manuscripts was sadly missing in the factory-made goods of the nineteenth century.

If John Ruskin offered the philosophical base for the Arts and Crafts movement, William Morris became its real world champion. During an incredibly productive life, Morris's influence on pottery, textiles, printing, glassblowing, metalwork, architecture and furniture was tremen-

dous. In 1861 he began a furniture guild that produced simple, handcrafted furniture and gradually established guilds in other crafts. In 1888 the Arts and Crafts Exhibition Society was formed, and shortly thereafter, the Arts and Crafts style was associated with handcrafted goods of all kinds.

## GUSTAV STICKLEY

Eventually Morris's influence spread across the ocean. In the 1890s, Gustav Stickley visited several British Arts and Crafts builders and returned to America imbued with the Arts and Crafts ideals. In 1899 he began a company in Syracuse, New York, producing furniture, metal-

work, lighting and textiles, eventually calling the company The Craftsman Workshops. He adopted the motto "Als ik kan," which means "as well as I am able," for his company. In 1901 he began to publish *The Craftsman*, a journal that articulated and spread the ideals of the Arts and Crafts movement to an eager American audience.

Stickley soon faced tremendous success. His mail-order furniture was gobbled up by eager buyers, and his ideas compelled other craftsmen to follow his lead. Unlike his English colleagues, Stickley did not reject machinery but felt that machines could spare the craftsmen from mindless drudgery and monotony, freeing them for more pleasure in the subtler hand skills of the craft and more consideration of design.

Stickley's adaptation of Ruskin's and Morris's ideas about honest, direct, straightforward furniture devoid of ornamentation meant that he built in quartersawn white oak, one of the strongest woods, and he used durable joinery, predominantly the exposed mortise and tenon joint. He used frame and panel construction where critical, although he preferred the more substantial look of solid wood construction. As exemplified by the photograph at the beginning of the chapter and the photographs at left and right, this sometimes made for massive furniture.

## HARVEY ELLIS AND ELBERT HUBBARD

Others, such as Harvey Ellis, softened and refined Stickley's heavy furniture until the elegance of Stickley's Craftsman style became established, as exemplified by the photograph of the clock on page 18.

Elbert Hubbard followed Stickley on a similar path to Arts and Crafts furniture. He visited William Morris in 1894 and returned to set up a series of shops devoted to printing and bookbinding. He named the shops "Roycroft" after two seventeenth-century bookbinders. Eventually, Hubbard began metalworking and woodworking shops, and, like Stickley, he sold his wares via catalog. His furniture remained faithful to the Gothic ideals he heard articulated by William Morris, but, to my eye at least, he never attained the graceful elegance of some of Stickley's later work and certainly nothing as successful as the Greene brothers' furniture.

## GREENE & GREENE

Charles and Henry Greene were born in Ohio and, in the 1890s, learned woodworking skills at the Manual Training School in St. Louis, Missouri, which was, by that time, thoroughly caught up in the Arts and Crafts fervor. Upon graduation from the Massachusetts Institute of Technology's architecture program in 1898, they went west to visit their parents who had retired to Pasadena, California. Along the way, they stopped at the Chicago World's Fair where they were first exposed to Japanese architectural elements. It was a fortuitous stop for them. Over the next 30 years, they combined the ideals of the Arts and Crafts movement with the Japanese and Chinese motifs they first saw in Chicago, and perhaps added a flavoring of the ecclesiastical furniture they found in the Spanish missions of the Southwest, to produce a unique take on the Arts and Crafts style. Initially, they worked in oak, like Stickley, and the stepped horizontal line they had seen in the oriental architecture in Chicago was prevalent in their earliest pieces. The pegged through tenon was predominant also; later, rounded corners and subtly curved transitions became their trademark.

## FURTHER DEVELOPMENTS

There were, of course, other makers in the Arts and Crafts style. Frank Lloyd Wright headed what was known as the Prairie School of the style. Charles Rennie Mackintosh was influential in Scotland and Canada. Stickley and the Greene brothers certainly exemplified the core of the Mission style in the United States.

By 1915 Gustav Stickley was bankrupt and the luster was gone from the Arts and Crafts movement, which was to be replaced by Modernism. Although the Greene brothers continued to build furniture into the 1930s, architecture was their main emphasis. Gustav's brothers

Photo by Alex Vertikoff

continued manufacturing Stickley's designs in upstate New York, but the woodworking world rather quickly slipped away from the ideals of William Morris.

Whether because of Stickley's early heavy furniture or because of the Greene brothers' exposure to the California missions, somehow the name "Mission" style became most prevalent for American Arts and Crafts furniture. In the end it doesn't matter what you call it. What does matter is that all of these builders remained true to Stickley's motto, "Als ik kan." And for this book, this is my motto as well.

Photo by Tim Street-Porter

## ❖ CUTTING THROUGH MORTISES

To rout through mortises for rails in legs, make a jig to appropriately locate the mortise holes and then route the mortises with a plunge router. Since Mission-style legs are thick, you will probably have to rout from both sides of the leg to make it all the way through.

Make sure the fence of the jig rests against the same face of the leg when you rout from opposite faces.

## ❖ CUTTING LEG MORTISES

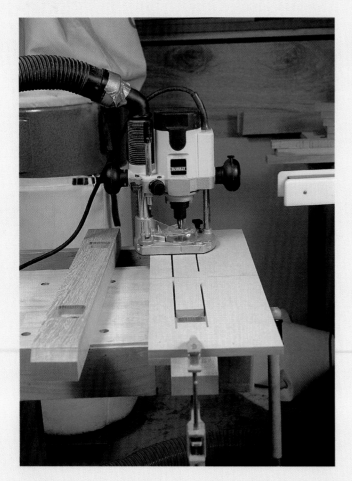

To cut the mortises in the feet for the legs to slide into, make a jig to locate the mortise holes on the feet and then rout the mortises with a plunge router with a template guide mounted on the baseplate.

# ❖ CUTTING SLAT MORTISES

You can build a jig that enables you to make a series of ½"-wide slots that are perfect for routing slat mortises in rails. Make two parallel saw cuts ⅝" apart on the table saw in a 6"-wide piece of medium density fiberboard (MDF). Then trim that to a 2"-long slot with a coping saw.

Attach a fence to the MDF parallel to the slot with drywall screws. Make sure the slot is centered on the workpiece. Use a ⅝" outer diameter (O.D.) template guide on the bottom of your plunge router and a ½" carbide upcut spiral bit to cut the ½"-wide slots in the slat mortising jig.

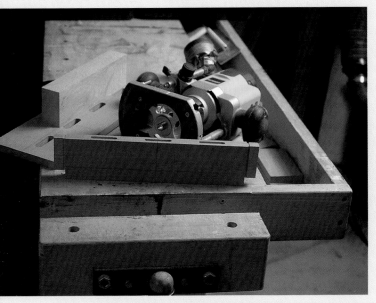

Three completed ¼"-wide slat mortises are simple to cut and you can rout a whole bunch of them in half an hour, if you're so inclined. I used a ¼" carbide upcut spiral bit and a ½" O.D. template guide.

In the same fashion, you can make a slat mortise routing jig in any multiple you need. Just remember, an odd number of slats is preferable from a design perspective. It's harder to make an even number of slats look right.

# ❖ MAKING QUADRALINEAR POSTS

The fixture for cutting the miter lock joint holds one leg piece vertically.

That piece is secured in the fixture with two drywall screws driven into the end grain of the workpiece at both ends.

The other edge of the fixture holds an identical leg piece horizontally.

The fixture holds the workpieces securely while routing a fairly big bite of wood and keeps your fingers away from the bit. I used a variable speed router set at the lowest rpm rate, in this case, 10,000 rpm.

Once all eight edges have been routed, the leg can be slipped together for a perfect Stickley leg with quartersawn faces showing on each outer surface.

## FINISHING ARTS AND CRAFTS FURNITURE

You've spent seven weekends building an extraordinary Arts and Crafts project, and it looks beautiful sitting there naked and unfinished. It's finely made, its joints are immaculately crafted, its lovely curves and proportions are perfect. All it needs is a coat of finish—right? Wrong. You're only half done, bud.

Any accomplished finisher will tell you that you need to spend as much time finishing a project as you do building it. And, if you can't do the time, you'd better prime, because the only one-coat finish you're likely to find is latex paint and even then you have to apply a primer coat. Wood finishing is the part of the craft that many woodworkers dread, and invariably, it's the most frequent source of failed woodworking. Why? Time. It simply takes more time than most novice and even intermediate woodworkers can believe.

The central problem of wood finishing is threefold: (1) you want the wood colored to the right tone or hue; (2) you want the wood protected; and (3) you want the wood to look its most beautiful. Determining the color of stain is an art form in which I have no skill. I'm simply not good with color. I get samples and show them to my wife, who is good with color. I am, however, able to make the right choices technically about stain. I've used all sorts—oil-based, water-based, gelled, and alcohol-based—and my favorite for oak has been the oil-based aniline dyes. I'm less experienced with mahogany, but I have had good results with oil-based wood stains on mahogany.

With regard to wood protection, there are basically two sorts of wood finish, the penetrating finish and the surface finish. The penetrating finishes, such as boiled linseed oil and tung oil, penetrate into the wood and change catalytically into a protective surface that resists penetration to some degree. It is a soft, low-luster finish, easy to apply and maintain. It has the advantage of being almost infinitely repairable. The surface finishes are also known as evaporative finishes, and they build up a hard coat of plastic film on the wood's surface, therefore protecting it more successfully against penetration by water, dirt and moisture. Surface finishes are more difficult to repair and can be produced in everything from a flat to a high-gloss sheen.

Which is more beautiful is in the eye of the beholder. I love the look of a high-luster, black lacquer piano, and nothing's more beautiful than a Nakashima bench with its oiled surface. Simply put, you need to know what you like in order to make the choice of what kind of finish you want.

Generally, the finishing process includes the following topics: repair, glue removal, scraping and sanding, filling, staining, finishing and rubbing out. I like to include another step in the process called planning. During the planning stage, I go through the entire sequence of the finishing process on scrap wood. I may be testing several different stains, fillers, techniques and finishes at the same time. If you are only a weekend woodworker, it may be several weeks before you even bring a brush near your completed but unfinished project. In conclu-

Touch the hot iron on the damp cloth to remove dents.

sion, I guess I could say, "Don't rush wood finishing."

## Repairing Wood

Let's start with repair. Inevitably during the construction stage of woodworking, you mar the wood. You inadvertently drop a chisel on it. You make mistakes. The wood chips out. The more experienced you are, the less this will happen. But the fact of the matter is, every project needs some repair. Two common repairs are dents and chips.

Repair gouges and wood splinters with instant glue as they occur.

### STEAMING OUT DENTS

Dents may be filled with wood filler, but try steaming them out first. On softer woods like mahogany, cover the dent with a damp cloth and then press a hot iron onto the cloth. Remove the cloth and observe the dent. The crushed wood fibers should have swollen somewhat from the steam. It may take several touches of the hot iron on the damp cloth to remove the dent, but I'm generally able to make the dent disappear with this trick.

### REPAIRING CHIPS

So the dent's gone. What to do about that edge where your router blew out an inch-long splinter of oak? I've become a great proponent of those instant glues that turners like so much. Whenever I have a blowout, I just collect the wood splinters and instant-glue them back in place right away. By attending to flaws in this way, right when they occur, I don't face huge numbers of flaws to repair at finishing time, and the flaws that I do find are smaller.

### FILLING FLAWS

OK, you've steamed out as many of the dents as you can, you've glued your index finger to your thumb and you're still faced with several flaws that need repair. Enter wood putty. There are many different brands of wood putty. Some are lacquer-based, some are oil-based, some harden, some do not. Some are stainable, some are prestained. Before you select a wood putty, you need to answer some questions.

1. What kind of finish do you want to apply?
2. Are the stain and the finish compatible with this sort of putty?
3. When do you want to apply this putty?

Given the answers, you should be able to select a wood putty that will perform adequately for you. Remember, however, that if you choose one of the prestained, nonhardening putties, you apply this putty between coats of plastic finish. If you apply it to a bare wood finish, this putty will bleed into the wood surrounding the flaw. This may be noticeable even after you apply a stain to it.

Some stainable putties accept stain after they've hardened, but many require you to mix stain into them prior to application. If so, mix stain into putty and apply it with a putty knife. If you have a large flaw, like a knot or crack, it may be necessary to apply several coats in order to build up a solid repair.

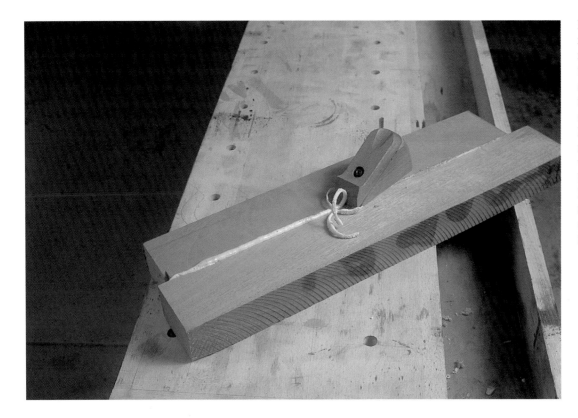

My little home-made chisel plane makes polyurethane glue squeeze-out easy to remove. If you can catch the yellow glue at just the right moment when it is dried but not completely hardened, you can zip off a string of squeeze-out easily.

When you've removed the mass of glue, attend to the surface with a cabinet scraper to remove the residual glue stains.

## Removing Glue

Glue "squeeze-out" is one of the banes of woodworking. I've never mastered the delicate touch of applying "just enough" glue, and I'm almost always faced with squeeze-out. Several tools are invaluable for dealing with this problem. First, my little selbstgemacht (homemade) chisel plane lets me peel off beads of glue in a relatively carefree manner. Long chisels also help, and the new polyurethane glues are much easier to remove than the old yellow glues. (On the other hand, if you can catch the yellow glue at just the right moment, when it is dried but not completely hardened, you can zip off a string of squeeze-out like it's cheese.)

When you've removed the mass of glue, attend to the surface with a cabinet scraper to remove the residual glue stains. Use of the cabinet scraper is an art form. Sharpened correctly, it is as fine a tool as a surgeon's scalpel; if sharpened incorrectly, it's more like an instrument of the Inquisition. Make sure your scraper's sharp.

## Scraping and Sanding

Scraping and sanding can overlap and intermingle with each of the other finishing processes, and there are also many times when scraping and sanding make sense during the construction of the project. Nonetheless, some scraping and sanding must occur after repair and glue removal and before staining or finishing, no matter how thoroughly you have sanded prior to these processes.

Scraping and sanding are two different solutions to the same condition. Your goal is to present clean, smooth surfaces to receive the wood finish. They arrive at that condition from somewhat different approaches—a scraped surface is a sheared surface; a sanded surface is an abraded one. This is to say that the scraped surface is analogous to a shaven face; you've sheared off any anomalies. With a sanded surface, you have arrived at a clear, smooth surface by rubbing successively finer and finer abrasives across that surface. Consequently, a scraped surface is burnished and unscratched, while a sanded surface is scratched with really fine scratches. In my ex-

perience, a scraped surface looks particularly good with a penetrating oil finish, while a closed-coat plastic finish looks best over a sanded surface.

In truth, I use both scraping and sanding in most of my finishing. I use scraping to remove material quickly without the danger of gouging or removing too much, but I use a belt sander where it makes sense, or where I must remove a lot of material fast. I depend on my little orbital sander for the great mass of my sanding efforts.

Regardless of which weapon I choose to sand with, I start out with the highest grade sandpaper I can, given the condition of the wood. Even though I buy S3S wood, all of the wood for my projects is planed again on my little portable planer that I take great care to maintain. Consequently, I don't have knife or roller marks to remove. I find I can begin with 120-grit sandpaper in

most circumstances, and I make 40-60-grit advancements through 220-grit sandpaper in order to prepare for staining and/or filling.

## Filling and Staining

Finishing oak is like painting pegboard—those holes are going to show no matter how much latex you brush on. Oak is one of the many ring-porous woods that woodworkers are faced with finishing. Ring-porous woods include elm, chestnut, pecan, hickory and ash. All need filler if you're going to apply a plastic-coated finish.

Grain filler compound looks like couscous or grits or gruel. It's thick, soupy stuff that you rub into the surface of the ring-porous woods to build up an even surface for the plastic film to span. Without filler, an oak surface with a plastic finish is lumpier than a New York street, and those lumps won't disappear no matter how many coats of finish you put on.

Grain filler compounds look like couscous or grits or gruel.

I always end up staining the oak first, letting it dry and then adding stain to the filler, but some have said that they just stain the filler. In my experience this never works, but if you want to try it, do so on your scrap trial pieces.

Use an old, stiff-bristled brush for applying the filler. Always have the paint store shake the can for you, as it's extremely difficult to remove lumps after sitting for a while on the shelf. Work in small sections at a time. Spread the filler on in accordance with the instructions on the can and wait for it to lose its glaze. To be efficient, just before it's set to lose its glaze, apply filler to another section and begin removing the section that's ready. Use burlap to remove the mass of the filler, rubbing the filler cross-grain into the exposed pores. You want to end up with filler in the pores, but you don't want a layer of filler hardened on top of the wood's surface, as it's like cement once hardened.

For the oak pieces of furniture in this book, I used Moser's aniline dye (oil soluble) in a medium-fumed oak color followed by two coats of boiled linseed oil rubbed in. Moser's stains are available from Woodworker's Supply. For those of you concerned with authenticity, read up on coloring oak with ammonia fumes in *Fine Woodworking,* Issue No. 120. I haven't fumed oak with any of these projects because the size of the fuming tent needed seemed prohibitive and I'm leery of the safety and health concerns about the process. For the mahogany pieces, I used a red mahogany oil-based stain from Minwax, followed by a polyurethane varnish, also from Minwax.

## Finishing

The grain is filled, you've stained, you've sanded. The wood stands before you perfectly prepared to receive a coat of finish. Vacuum and use a tack cloth to remove any debris from your perfect surface. If you've filled the pores on oak, now is the time to apply finish. If you have used some other wood, you may need a sealer coat. Buy an appropriate sealer for your finish, or dilute your finish with an appropriate solvent if so recommended on the can. Apply the finish with a good brush (have a brush appropriate to the finish that you use only for that finish). Don't use the same brush you use for painting your house—rather, pay attention to the characteristics of the finish you're applying, and use an appropriately sized brush with the best tip shape for the job.

Between coats, lightly sand with the orbital sander or by hand with 220 paper, and remove the inevitable flaws with a razor blade. Sand back to a perfect surface, but not through the coat you've just applied. I use mineral spirits as a lubricant in the 300- and 400-grit range of sandpaper. After three coats of finish, I begin using fine steel wool, again lubricated with mineral spirits. If the finish is thick enough, I will use steel wool lubricated with beeswax to rub out the finish to the desired gloss.

Between coats, sand lightly with the orbital sander or by hand with 220-grit paper, and remove the inevitable flaws with a razor blade.

# ❖ CHARACTERISTIC DETAILS OF ARTS AND CRAFTS FURNITURE

Nowadays, you can spot Arts and Crafts furniture just about anywhere. It shows up in television shows, commercials and movies. Many magazines beyond woodworking magazines show Mission-style or Craftsman-style furniture in their articles and advertisements. And you can usually expect to see something on *The Antiques Roadshow* on PBS. But how does one recognize Arts and Crafts furniture without someone telling them what it is?

There are a number of different structural and aesthetic details that are commonly tied to Arts and Crafts furniture or its subgroups (Mission, Craftsman, Prairie, Greene & Greene, etc.). The following characteristic details, while not necessarily exclusive to Arts and Crafts furniture, are generally attributed to such and can easily guide the novice in finding the pieces they seek or help them construct pieces as an homage to the style or one of its proponents.

## Simple Lines

The Arts and Crafts movement of England is generally considered to have been started by William Morris and John Ruskin as a reaction against the seemingly uninspired and mechanically created furniture of the Industrial Revolution. It was also a reaction against garish Victorian designs and frills. In general, for both the English and American Arts and Crafts movement, the styles, designs and construction of furniture harkened back to days when craftsmen built furniture with great skill and care and when designs were dictated more by pragmatism and craftsmanship than pure aesthetics. Beauty was seen as an extension of practical design and sturdy craftsmanship.

So, in reaction to frilly ornamentation of Victorian furniture and to its mechanized—and often shoddy—construction, Arts and Crafts furniture manifested itself in simple lines and simple joinery. While an honest-to-goodness William Morris Morris chair looks different from a Stickley Morris chair, they both feature simple, straight lines with little, if any, ornamentation.

Perhaps the greatest expression of simple lines is found in Frank Lloyd Wright's Prairie-style furniture, similar to the "cube" chair shown in the photograph below. Wright's designs employed simple geometric figures and sweeping horizontal lines to attract the eye without "cluttering" the image. Simple geometry and natural motifs are common throughout much of what is considered Arts and Crafts style, and modern builders can successfully employ them in re-creations and original pieces inspired by the movement.

This Wright-inspired chair demonstrates the simplicity of design found in simple geometric forms: the straight lines of the spindles and the square, flat back and arms.

## CORBELS

A corbel is one of the few embellishments found in Arts and Crafts furniture. While it is used in some applications as a structural element to support some joints and members, it is most often simply decorative. Mission and Craftsman furniture (if you can or must make a distinction) employ corbels in a wide variety of applications—on chairs, settles, lamps, tables, stands and much more. Described simply, a corbel is a kind of bracket or support, much like a buttress of a building, which connects a horizontal member to a vertical member with a long, gentle curve (as shown in the photograph below and drawing at right.) Despite its primarily aesthetic role, it complements the design with its simple curve, often tying into pieces that have an occasional curve in their component parts, such as an apron in a chair or table.

A corbel can vary in length, width and direction (many lamps and other stands use it coming from the base and along the uprights).

Even the makers of this Arts and Crafts knockoff rocker were careful to duplicate corbels below the arms of the chair.

## SIMPLE JOINERY

While many pieces of furniture are valued for intricate joinery, such as dovetail or pin and crescent joints, Arts and Crafts furniture, being a response to busy design and complicated construction, is valued for its simple joinery. The vast majority of all Arts and Crafts furniture is constructed using simple mortise and tenon joints or some variation on them. Considering that a lot of Stickley's furniture was so massive and rectilinear, it makes sense that he would employ such a strong and simple joint such as a mortise and tenon.

Through tenons held in place with "tusks" or pins made assembly and disassembly easy and became characteristic of many Craftsman and Mission-style furniture pieces. In fact, many through tenons, particularly in stile-and-rail case pieces, became more aesthetic in purpose rather than pragmatic. Take, for example, the through tenon in the arm of the chair pictured on this page. While it wasn't absolutely necessary to make it a through tenon, it was probably easier to do so, and it provides an interesting visual, as well as tactile, detail.

Using simple joinery is also a bonus to the modern craftsman, whether skilled or inexperienced. It is simple to learn and quick to employ with either powered or unpowered tools.

This Arts-and-Crafts-inspired taboret features simple half-lap and "tusked" or pinned through mortise and tenon joints.

The through tenon of the leg through the arm of this rocker makes a nice tactile detail.

## CLOUD LIFT

The cloud lift is not widespread among a lot of different Arts and Crafts styles; it is usually restricted to Greene & Greene style furniture. In their travels, the Greene brothers came into contact with Japanese style furniture and design and became enamored with it. While still of the same "simple design and construction" mindset of the Arts and Crafts movement of their day, they added some of the design elements and construction practices they found in various forms of oriental furniture. The cloud lift is one of those elements.

Strictly an embellishment, the cloud lift serves as a visual relief, breaking up and softening horizontal lines. It is used many times in rails and stretchers, as in the back rail of the garden bench pictured here at bottom right. It is also used in shorter applications, such as in the feet of the Greene & Greene inspired cradle at bottom left. Basically, the element comes from oriental designs and is reminiscent of layers of clouds or rolling hills, again tying into the simple lines, geometric figures and natural motifs found in many Arts and Crafts pieces.

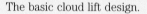

The basic cloud lift design.

The feet of this Greene & Greene inspired cradle would have been entirely too bulky if left square, but the cloud lift allows for more mass in the feet without appearing clunky.

Even though this garden bench seems to be long and flowing, the cloud lift details in the back rail make the design more organic and pleasing to the eye.

## KNOCKDOWN JOINERY

As Gustav Stickley expanded his Craftsman efforts, one of his endeavors was *The Craftsman* magazine. In *The Craftsman*, Stickley championed the home craftsman and simple living, both of which fit very well with his Craftsman line of furniture, which is simple in design and of knockdown construction, so that it can be assembled by the buyer.

Many furniture companies of the time took advantage of knockdown construction. Consider reading a catalog or perhaps an advertisement in a magazine in search of a nice Mission-style settle for the living room. Sure, the cost of the piece itself might be right, but if it has to be shipped across the country by train, the shipping charges may be prohibitive. Since many manufacturers needed to reach a market wider than their immediate geographical location, it made sense to try to reduce shipping costs. Freight cars are only so big, and a fully constructed, crated settle will take up a lot more space than a settle that is broken down into component parts that can easily be reconstructed by the consumer.

Now, while most people don't purchase a lot of furniture through mail-order catalogs these days, our society keeps many of us repeatedly moving from house to house; so knockdown furniture still has its bonuses. With the innovations of hardware manufacturers and furniture builders, even the most complicated piece of furniture has the potential for being built in such a way that it can be taken apart quickly and easily. The bed-frame hardware used on the settle in chapter two is an example of modern innovation meeting historic application.

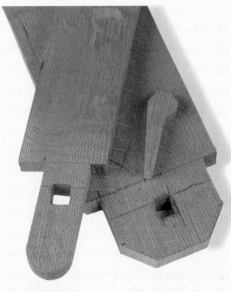

These through tenons with mortises for pins allow the taboret (above) to be quickly and easily taken apart and reconstructed.

Bed-rail fasteners allow the settle to be knockdown in construcion without losing the smooth lines of the design.

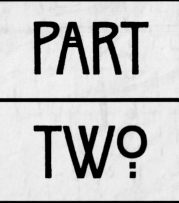

# PART TWO:

Stickley's statement, taken from a hammered copper fireplace hood at his Craftsman Farm, expresses one of his personal goals in seeking the "good life," that of fine craftsmanship and skilled work. This phrase, reminiscent of days gone by, seems as if it were taken from some medieval text on woodworking.

"THE LYF SO SHORT, THE CRAFT
SO LONG TO LERNE."

—SLOGAN FROM CRAFTSMAN FARMS,
GUSTAV STICKLEY

# THE LIVING ROOM

Those of you who've read *The Hobbit* will no doubt remember the first paragraph that describes the homes the hobbits lived in:

> *"In a hole in the ground there lived a hobbit. Not*
> *a nasty, dirty, wet hole, filled with the ends of*
> *worms and an oozy smell, nor yet a dry, bare,*
> *sandy hole with nothing in it to sit down on or to*
> *eat: it was a hobbit-hole, and that means comfort."*

In this brief description, J.R.R. Tolkien pretty much describes an Arts-and-Crafts-style living room, too; just look at that Morris chair and ottoman, and tell me you don't want to plunk down in it, put your feet up and dream of adventures.

Now this particular variant of the genus is the West Coast version; I've built the six pieces of furniture with a Greene & Greene flavor. You'll note I've used mahogany and that the legs carry a slight oriental flavor. Further, the ramrod-straight, no-nonsense lines shown in Stickley's pieces have been softened with gentle curves and rounded, rather than beveled, edges. The vertical line defined by the use of slats is still prevalent, and the honest, chunky heaviness—characteristic of the style—still dominates; but the Greene & Greene pieces, as a rule, seem lighter and more graceful.

Because of these differences, I've included a sidebar to help you deal with shaping the legs. For the finish, I used Minwax's Red Mahogany stain with a polyurethane semigloss finish.

# THE MORRIS CHAIR

I f one piece of furniture defines the Arts and Crafts style, it is the Morris chair. Named for William Morris, it's had more lives than Morris the Cat. I've seen more varied renditions of the Morris chair coast to coast and north to south than just about any other piece of furniture. I've seen it rustic, refined and even as a rocker, but here I've tried to build it in congruence with the West Coast ideals of the Arts and Crafts style.

This particular chair was inspired by a chair I saw in the book *In the Arts and Crafts Style* and was originally built by the Berkeley Mill and Furniture Company. I modified the chair significantly, however. First, and probably most important, I used bed-rail fastener hardware to fasten the front and rear rails to the side leg assemblies. Another difference was using a metal rod as a pivot mechanism on which the seat back rotates. There are other subtler differences you'll probably note when you study the drawing, but like most Morris chairs, it's a good sitting chair if you can keep the cat out of it.

## BUILDING THE MORRIS CHAIR

*Step 1.* Select wood and match grain patterns. Mill wood flat, square and to size.

**MATERIALS LIST**

### The Morris Chair

| NAME | NO. REQ'D | THICKNESS | WIDTH | LENGTH |
|------|-----------|-----------|-------|--------|
| Leg | 4 | 3½″ | 3½″ | 20″ |
| Upper Side Rail | 2 | 1″ | 3″ | 28″ |
| Lower Side Rail | 2 | 1″ | 6″ | 28″ |
| Front Rail | 1 | 1″ | 6″ | 23½″ |
| Rear Rail | 1 | 1″ | 5″ | 23½″ |
| Side Slat | 10 | ½″ | 2½″ | 7″ |
| Back Stile | 2 | 1″ | 2½″ | 24″ |
| Back Rail | 2 | 1″ | 3½″ | 22″ |
| Back Slat | 3 | ½″ | 3½″ | 18″ |
| Arm | 2 | 1″ | 5″ | 33″ |
| Arm Rail | 1 | 1″ | 1¾″ | 28¾″ |

Front View

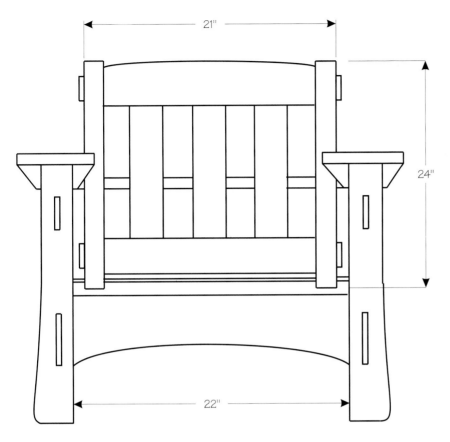

Side View

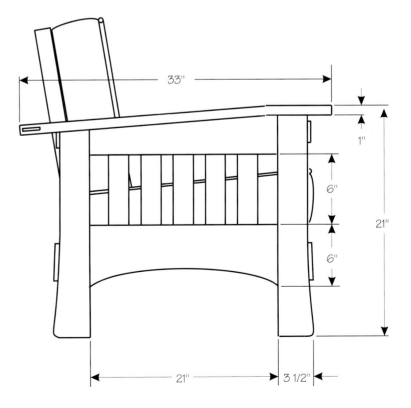

## Arm Assembly

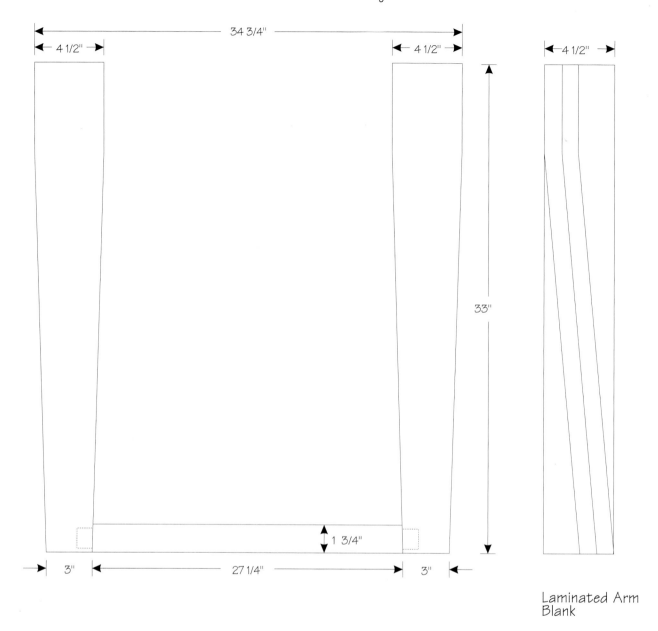

Laminated Arm
Blank

# ❖ DRAWING A CURVE

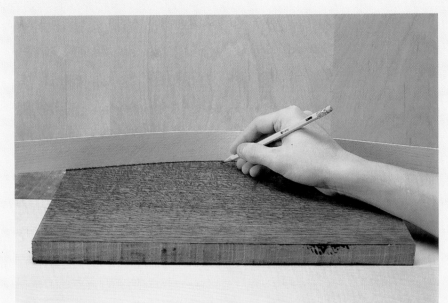

In order to get the 1½″-deep curve on the front and back seat rails, you will need a ⅛″-thick fiberboard batten about 1″ wide and at least 26″ long. Tack a finishing nail near the bottom edge of both ends of the rail about 11⅛″ from the center of the rail. Tack another finishing nail into the center of the rail about 1½″ from the bottom edge. Bend the batten to form a curve, using the nails to hold it in place. Draw the curve along the batten.

*Step 2.* Laminate 8/4 pieces for leg blanks and arms. Mill leg blanks square and to size.

*Step 3.* Determine which faces of the leg blanks should face out; mark mortise positions. Rout the ½″ through mortises using the jig shown on page 20. Chop the mortises square with a mortising chisel.

*Step 4.* Trace the pattern's shape onto two adjacent faces; check that mortises are in the right place. (See the sidebar "Shaping the Legs" on page 42.) Saw the pattern you drew on two surfaces of the leg blank.

*Step 5.* Clamp the pattern in place. Rout the shape onto the rough-sawn faces of the leg.

*Step 6.* Sand the shape smooth with a bearing-guided drum sander mounted in the drill press. Finish sanding with a pneumatic sanding drum or by hand.

*Step 7.* Rout the edges round with a ¼″-radius roundover bit along all straight edges. Round the curved edges to match the ¼″-radius cut by using a router with a cabinetmaker's rasp and hand sanding.

*Step 8.* Cut side-rail tenons to size by best available means—I used a tenoning jig on the table saw. Fit tenons to mortises. Bevel tenon ends with the router, cut rail curve on band saw, and sand the curved edges with drum sander.

*Step 9.* Cut slat mortises using the jig and technique shown on page 21.

*Step 10.* Assemble legs and rails without glue.

*Step 11.* Use the leg/rail assembly to determine final slat length. Trim slats to final size and cut stub tenons on slat ends. Bevel slat edges and round over the curved rail edges with the router using the ¼″-radius roundover bit.

*Step 12.* Stain and apply one coat of finish to the slats and the edges of the rails to which the mortises have been cut.

*Step 13.* Insert the slats into the rails dry, then slide the rail tenons into the leg mortises with an appropriate adhesive; I used Titebond polyurethane glue. Clamp overnight.

*Step 14.* Using the method described in the sidebar "Drawing a Curve," draw the radius arc on the front and rear rails. Cut the long arcs

# ❖ SHAPING THE LEGS

After cutting the through mortises in both sides of the squared leg blank, use the MDF patterns to lay out the leg's shape.

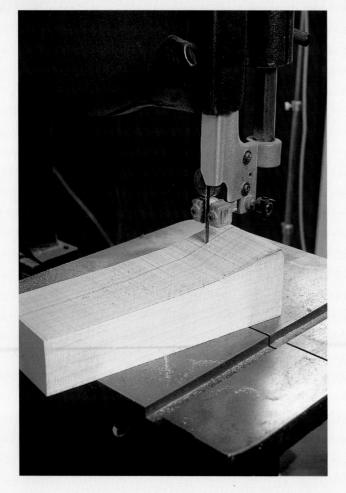

Band saw the leg's rough shape. Make sure the saw-kerf is sawn slightly on the outside of the pencil line.

Clamp the pattern on the leg so that the fence is against a straight face of the leg and the curved portion of the pattern is almost aligned with the sawn face. Copy the pattern's exact shape onto the rough-sawn face of the leg with a pattern bit chucked in your router.

Sand the rough-sawn face smooth with a bearing-guided drum sander mounted in a drill press. The bearing rides along the smooth surface you established with your pattern bit in the previous step.

Use an inflatable drum sander to smooth the leg to final shape.

This process allows even old gaffers like me to turn out multiples of this shapely little leg.

on the band saw or with a saber saw. Sand the arcs and round over the edges with the router using the ¼"-radius roundover bit.

*Step 15.* Rout the recess for the bed-rail fasteners (The Woodworkers' Store, part No. 28589) in the legs and rails. Screw the bed-rail fasteners in place and assemble the rails and sides.

*Step 16.* Locate the axle holes on the rear legs, disassemble and bore the ⅜" holes for the seat back axle (⅜"-dia. steel rod).

*Step 17.* Lay out the angled cut at the top of the side assemblies. Cut the top angle on each of the side assemblies on the band saw.

*Step 18.* Mill the laminated material for the arms square. Use the cutoff portion of the side as a pattern to establish the angle to be cut on the laminated arm blank. Band saw two arms from the laminated blank. Plane and sand the arms to size and shape. Draw arm shape from the pattern on page 40. Band saw, plane, and sand arm to shape.

*Step 19.* Rout ¼" mortises, 1" deep on inside edge of each arm. Chop mortises square with chisel. Cut tenons on rear arm rail with tenoning jig on the table saw. Fit tenon to mortise. Glue tenons and assemble arm assembly. (I used Titebond polyurethane glue.) Clamp overnight.

*Step 20.* Round over the upper arm assembly edges.

*Step 21.* Reassemble the rails and sides and then position the arm assembly in place.

*Step 22.* Bore four ⅜" holes halfway through the arm assembly on center with the legs. Bore ⅛" holes on center with the ⅜" holes all the way through the arm assembly.

*Step 23.* Bore ⅜" holes through the bottom edge of the back stiles. Cut ¼"-wide mortises, 1" deep in position at the top and bottom of the stiles. Chop these mortises square with a chisel. Cut tenons to fit the ¼"-wide mortises on the table saw with a tenoning jig on the rail members.

*Step 24.* Lay out and cut the curved shape of the top rail on the band saw. Sand the band-sawn edges smooth and bevel with a beveling bit in a router.

*Step 25.* Cut the tenons on the upper stile members using a tenoning jig on the table saw.

*Step 26.* Rout the slat mortises in the upper and lower back rails using the jig and technique shown in chapter one.

*Step 27.* As earlier with the side slats, assemble the back, determine proper slat length and cut the stub tenons. Glue the tenons in the lower rails, slide them into their respective

mortises and then position the nine slats in place. Glue the stile tenons and slide the upper rail in place, fitting the upper slat tenons into their mortises. Dry and clamp the back assembly; leave overnight.

*Step 28.* Sand each assembly through 180-grit sandpaper and finish with three coats of polyurethane. Reassemble the rails to the sides.

*Step 29.* Rip enough 1×1 scrap hardwood to fit around the inside perimeter of the rails. Drill ⅛" holes every 10" in these pieces of scrap, and countersink each hole. Trim the scrap to fit around the inside perimeter of the rail, 2" down from the top rail edges.

*Step 30.* Cut a piece of ¾" plywood to fit between the rails and sides, notching out the corners to allow for the leg.

*Step 31.* Paint the steel rod a complementary color, then assemble the completed Morris chair. Screw 1¼" long drywall screws through the ⅜" holes in the arms and into the legs.

*Step 32.* Use ⅜" mahogany buttons to plug the holes. Trim, sand and finish these buttons so that they are invisible (see sidebar "Gluing in Buttons" on page 53).

*Step 33.* Have upholstery done.

# THE OTTOMAN

I f you're going to build the Morris chair and/or the settle, I'd recommend you begin here with the ottoman, because it's a simpler project, and you will soon learn the techniques for making the shaped foot, which is central to making any of the other projects in this chapter. The building goes pretty fast, too, so it's the kind of project that you can do in a weekend.

In essence, the shaping of the foot is an exercise in pattern routing with some judicious power sanding thrown in for good measure, and because you've cut the mortises prior to the shaping, you can be confident that the project will be square and true once assembled. It's a good feeling and a great little project.

**MATERIALS LIST**

## *The Ottoman*

| NAME | NO. REQ'D | THICKNESS | WIDTH | LENGTH |
|---|---|---|---|---|
| Leg | 4 | 3½″ | 3½″ | 11″ |
| Side Rail | 2 | 1″ | 6″ | 23″ |
| Front and Back Rail | 2 | 1″ | 6″ | 18″ |
| Gusset | 4 | 1″ | 4″ | 4″ |

## BUILDING THE OTTOMAN

*Step 1.* Select wood and match grain patterns. Mill wood flat, square and to size.

*Step 2.* Laminate 8/4 pieces for leg blanks. Mill leg blanks square and to size.

*Step 3.* Determine which faces of the leg blanks should face out; mark mortise positions. Rout the ½" through mortises using the jig shown in the process on page 20. Chop the mortises square with a mortising chisel.

*Step 4.* Trace the pattern's shape onto two adjacent faces; check that mortises are in the right place. (See "Shaping the Legs" sidebar on page 42.) Saw the pattern you drew on two surfaces of the leg blank.

*Step 5.* Clamp the pattern in place. Rout the shape onto the rough-sawn faces of the leg. Sand the shape smooth with a bearing-guided drum sander mounted in the drill press.

*Step 6.* Finish sanding with a pneumatic sanding drum or by hand.

*Step 7.* Rout the edges round with a ¼"-radius roundover bit along all straight edges. Round the curved edges to match the ¼"-radius cut by using a router with a cabinetmaker's rasp and hand sanding.

*Step 8.* Cut side-rail tenons to size by best available means; I used a tenoning jig on the table saw. Fit tenons to mortises.

*Step 9.* Lay out curves on rails. Cut curves on band saw. Sand curves with drum sander.

*Step 10.* Round over rail edges with a ¼" roundover bit mounted in a router.

*Step 11.* Glue tenons with polyurethane glue; assemble ottoman.

*Step 12.* Cut gussets, glue and install with drywall screws. Sand, stain and finish. Cut a rectangular piece of plywood to fit over the gussets and serve as a base for the cushion and upholstery. After the cushion has been finished, screw drywall screws through the gussets and into the plywood base for a secure and good-looking ottoman.

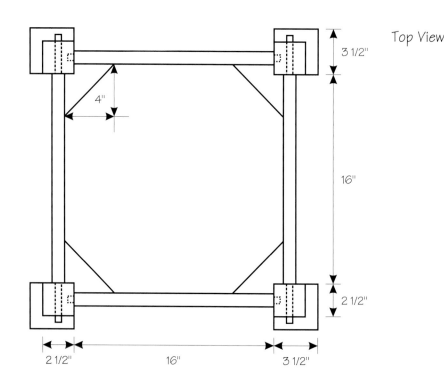

Top View

4"

3 1/2"

16"

2 1/2"

2 1/2"    16"    3 1/2"

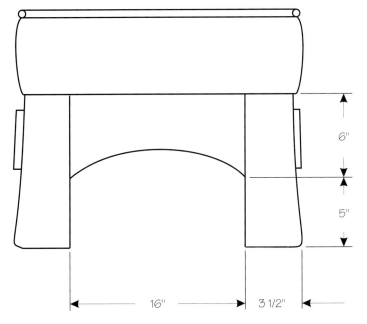

Side View

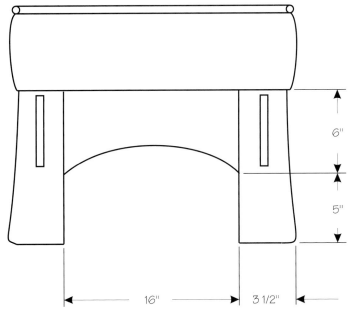

Front View

# THE SETTLE

I've never seen this settle anywhere else, but it seems a logical progression from the Morris chair I built. Like the Morris chair, I've used bed-rail fasteners to make the settle secure enough for even well-fed and full-sized Victorian gentlemen to sit. Also, like the Morris chair, the back of this settle pivots on a 66"-long, ⅜" metal rod, and it rests against the rear arm rail, which is mortised and tenoned into the two arms.

## BUILDING THE SETTLE

*Step 1.* Select wood and match grain patterns. Mill wood flat, square and to size.

*Step 2.* Laminate 8/4 pieces for leg

**MATERIALS LIST**

### The Settle

| NAME | NO. REQ'D | THICKNESS | WIDTH | LENGTH |
|---|---|---|---|---|
| Leg | 4 | 3½" | 3½" | 20" |
| Upper Side Rail | 2 | 1" | 3" | 28" |
| Lower Side Rail | 2 | 1" | 6" | 28" |
| Front Rail | 1 | 1" | 6" | 67½" |
| Rear Rail | 1 | 1" | 5" | 67½" |
| Side Slat | 10 | ½" | 2½" | 7" |
| Back Stile | 4 | 1" | 2½" | 24" |
| Back Rail | 6 | 1" | 3½" | 19" |
| Back Slat | 9 | ½" | 3½" | 19" |
| Arm | 2 | 1" | 5" | 33" |
| Arm Rail | 1 | 1" | 1¾" | 68" |

| HARDWARE | PART NO. | NO. REQ'D | SUPPLIER |
|---|---|---|---|
| Bed-Rail Fastener | 28589 | 1 set | The Woodworkers' Store |
| Center Rail Rastener | 10025 | 1 set | The Woodworkers' Store |
| ⅜"-dia. Steel Rod | | 1 | Any hardware store |

Front View

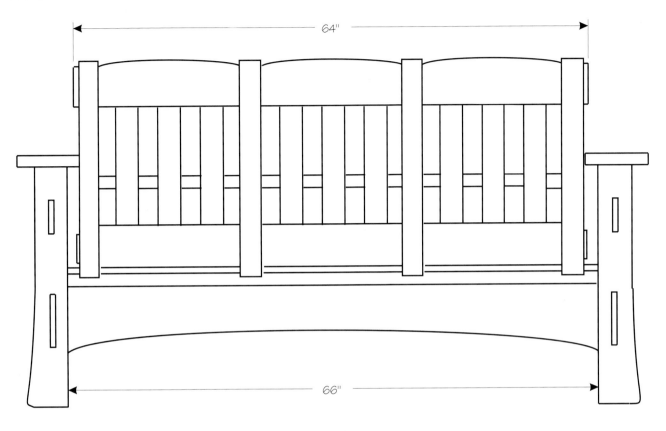

64"

66"

Side View

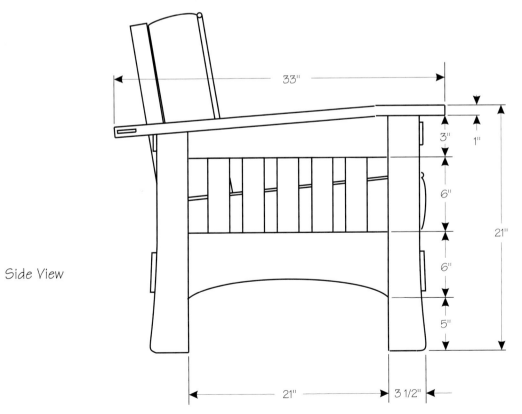

33"

3"

1"

6"

21"

6"

5"

21"

3 1/2"

blanks and arms. Mill leg blanks square and to size.

*Step 3.* Determine which faces of the leg blanks should face out; mark mortise positions. Rout the ½" through mortises using the process on page 20. Chop the mortises square with a mortising chisel.

*Step 4.* Trace the pattern's shape onto two adjacent faces; check that mortises are in the right place. Saw the pattern you drew on two surfaces of the leg blank.

*Step 5.* Clamp the pattern in place. Rout the shape onto the rough-sawn faces of the leg. Sand the shape smooth with a bearing-guided drum sander mounted in the drill press. Finish sanding with a pneumatic sanding drum or by hand.

*Step 6.* Rout the edges round with a ¼"-radius roundover bit along all straight edges. Round the curved edges to match the ¼"-radius cut by using a router with a cabinetmaker's rasp and hand sanding.

*Step 7.* Cut side-rail tenons to size by best available means; I used a tenoning jig on the table saw. Fit tenons to mortises. Bevel tenon ends with the router, cut rail curve on band saw and sand the curved edges with drum sander.

*Step 8.* Cut slat mortises using the jig and technique shown on page 21.

*Step 9.* Assemble legs and rails without glue.

*Step 10.* Use the leg/rail assembly to determine final slat length. Trim slats to final size; cut stub tenons on slat ends. Bevel slat edges and round

over the curved rail edges with the router using the ¼"-radius round-over bit.

*Step 11.* Stain and apply one coat of finish to the slats and the edges of the rails to which the mortises have been cut.

*Step 12.* Insert the slats into the rails dry, then slide the rail tenons into the leg mortises with an appro-

priate adhesive; I used Titebond polyurethane glue. Clamp and leave overnight.

*Step 13.* Using the method described in the sidebar "Drawing a Curve" on page 41, draw the radius arc on the front and rear rails. Cut the long arcs on the band saw or with a saber saw. Sand the arcs and round over the edges with the router using

the ¼″-radius roundover bit.

*Step 14.* Rout the recess for the bed-rail fasteners in the legs and rails. Screw the bed-rail fasteners in place and assemble the rails and sides.

*Step 15.* Locate the axle holes on the rear legs, disassemble and bore the ⅜″ holes for the seat back axle.

*Step 16.* Lay out the angled cut at the top of the side assemblies. Cut the top angle on each of the side assemblies on the band saw.

*Step 17.* Mill the laminated material for the arms square. Use the cutoff portion of the side as a pattern to establish the angle to be cut on the laminated arm blank. Band saw two arms from the laminated blank. Plane and sand the arms to size and shape.

*Step 18.* Draw arm shape from pattern on page 42. Band saw, plane and sand arm to shape.

*Step 19.* Rout ¼″ mortises 1″ deep on inside edge of each arm. Chop mortises square with chisel.

*Step 20.* Cut tenons on rear arm rail with tenoning jig on the table saw. Fit tenon to mortise. Glue tenons and assemble arm assembly. I used Titebond polyurethane glue. Clamp and leave overnight.

*Step 21.* Round over the upper arm assembly edges. Reassemble the rails and sides, and then position the arm assembly in place.

*Step 22.* Bore four ⅜″ holes halfway through the arm assembly on center with the legs. Bore ⅛″ holes on center with the ⅜″ holes all the way through the arm assembly.

*Step 23.* Bore ⅜″ holes through the bottom edge of the back stiles. Cut ¼″-wide mortises, 1″ deep in position at the bottom of the stiles. Chop these mortises square with a chisel. Cut tenons to fit the ¼″-wide mortises on the table saw with a tenoning jig on the three lower back-rail members.

*Step 24.* Cut the three through mortises into the top back rail. (I could only rout about 1¼″ deep from each edge and, consequently, I used a ³⁄₁₆″ twist bit and drilled out much of the waste from the mortise in the 3″-wide stock. I then cleaned up the remainder with a chisel.) Chop the mortises square with a chisel.

*Step 25.* Lay out and cut the

curved shape of the top rail on the band saw. Sand the band-sawn edges smooth and bevel with a beveling bit in a router.

*Step 26.* Cut the tenons on the upper stile members using a tenoning jig on the table saw.

*Step 27.* Rout the slat mortises in the upper and lower back rails using the jig and technique shown on page 21. As earlier with the side slats, assemble the back, determine proper slat length and cut the stub tenons. Glue the tenons in the lower rails, slide them into their respective mortises and then position the nine slats in place. Glue the stile tenons; slide the upper rail in place, fitting the up-

per slat tenons into their mortises. Dry, clamp the back assembly and leave overnight.

*Step 28.* Sand each assembly through 180-grit sandpaper and finish with three coats of polyurethane.

*Step 29.* Reassemble the rails to the sides. Install center rail fasteners by screwing them to the inside faces of the front and rear rails so that the wooden support will be 2″ down from the upper edge of the rail. Cut two 2 × 4 supports to fit into the center rail fasteners. Rip enough 1 × 1 scrap hardwood to fit around the inside perimeter of the rails. Drill ⅛″ holes every 10″ in these pieces of scrap and countersink each hole.

Trim the scrap to fit around the inside perimeter of the rail, 2″ down from the top rail edges.

*Step 30.* Cut a piece of ¾″ plywood to fit between the rails and sides, notching out the corners to allow for the leg.

*Step 31.* Paint the steel rod a complementary color, then assemble the complete settle.

*Step 32.* Screw 1¼″-long drywall screws through the ⅜″ holes in the arms and into the legs. Use ⅜″ mahogany buttons to plug the holes; trim, sand and finish these buttons so that they are invisible.

Arm Assembly

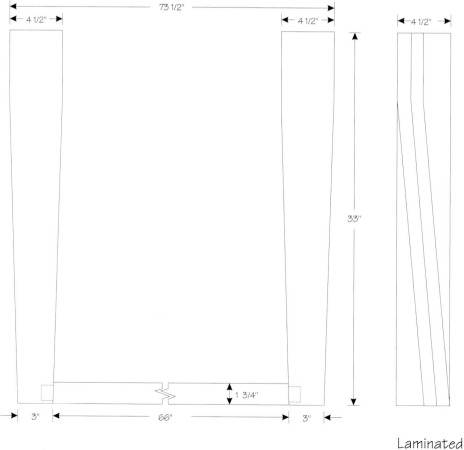

73 1/2″

4 1/2″      4 1/2″      4 1/2″

33″

3″      66″      3″

1 3/4″

Laminated Arm Blank

## ❖ GLUING IN BUTTONS

Glue in mahogany buttons with polyurethane glue.

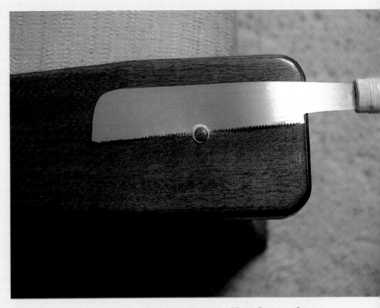

After the glue dries, trim off excess button. Here I use a Japanese flush-cut saw to trim the button flush with the chair's arm.

You can also use a sharp chisel to pare the button flush.

Sand lightly through 220-grit sandpaper.

Apply stain with a small brush. Apply finish, sanding between coats until a smooth finish is realized.

# THE END TABLE

I must confess that I've built many variations of this stately little end table, mostly scaled-down adaptations of Stickley's library table in oak, but occasionally in cherry and even in poplar when the customer wanted a pair of painted tables. However, this is the first end table I've made in mahogany. It was, of course, Greene & Greene inspired, and you'll no doubt recognize the changes that make it so: the curved rather than beveled edges, the shaped feet and the curved rails.

## BUILDING THE END TABLE

*Step 1.* Select wood and match grain patterns. Mill wood straight, square and to thickness.

*Step 2.* Glue up panels wide enough for the top.

*Step 3.* Laminate 8/4 pieces for leg blanks. Mill leg blanks square and to size.

*Step 4.* Determine which faces of the leg blanks should face out; mark mortise positions. Rout the ½″ through mortises and the 1″-deep mortises using the process shown on page 20. Chop the mortises square with a mortising chisel.

*Step 5.* Trace the pattern's shape onto two adjacent faces; check that

MATERIALS LIST

## The End Table

| NAME | NO. REQ'D | THICKNESS | WIDTH | LENGTH |
|------|-----------|-----------|-------|--------|
| Top | 1 | ¾″ | 20½″ | 29½″ |
| Leg | 4 | 2½″ | 2½″ | 19¾″ |
| Upper End Rail | 2 | 1″ | 2¾″ | 13″ |
| Lower End Rail | 2 | 1″ | 4″ | 13″ |
| Upper Side Rail | 2 | 1″ | 2¾″ | 28″ |
| Lower Side Rail | 2 | 1″ | 4″ | 28″ |
| Slat | 6 | ⅜″ | 2½″ | 8″ |
| Shelf | 1 | ¾″ | 13½″ | 24½″ |

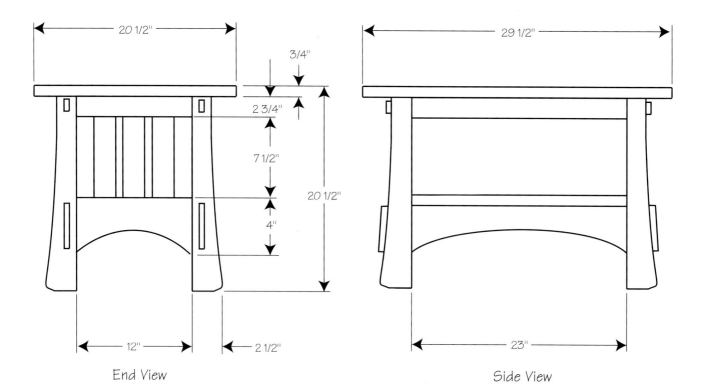

End View

Side View

Leg Pattern

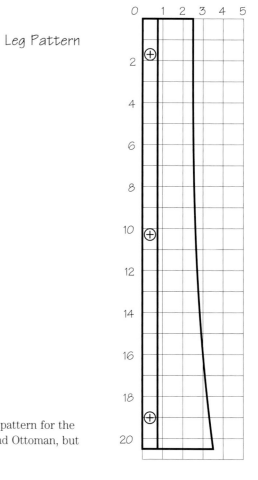

Use the same shaped pattern for the Morris chair, Settle and Ottoman, but one inch wider.

mortises are in the right place. Saw the pattern you drew on two surfaces of the leg blank on the band saw.

*Step 6.* Clamp the pattern in place. Rout the shape onto the rough-sawn faces of the leg. Sand the shape smooth with a bearing-guided drum sander mounted in the drill press. Finish sanding with a pneumatic sanding drum or by hand.

*Step 7.* Rout the edges round with a ¼″-radius roundover bit along all straight edges. Round the curved edges to match the ¼″-radius cut by using a router with a cabinetmaker's rasp and hand sanding.

*Step 8.* Surface and sand the top to final thickness. Rip and crosscut the top to final size.

*Step 9.* Bevel the edges of the top with a beveling bit mounted in a router.

*Step 10.* Mill rail and slat material to size and thickness. Cut tenons on the table saw with a tenoning jig. Fit tenons to mortises. Bevel tenon ends, slat edges.

*Step 11.* Rout slat mortises. Cut slat tenons on the table saw with a tenoning jig. Chop rounded ends of slat mortises square with chisel. Fit slat tenons to mortises.

*Step 12.* Round over curved rail edges using a ball-bearing-guided ¼″-radius roundover bit in your router. Bevel the straight rail edges.

*Step 13.* Sand, stain and apply two coats of finish to the rail edges that have the slat mortises cut in them, and do the same with the slats.

*Step 14.* Assemble the two end table ends by fitting the slats in place (without glue) and then gluing and clamping the four end rails in place. After the glue has dried, scrape any

squeeze-out and sand the side assemblies.

*Step 15.* Assemble the end table frame by inserting the slats into each of their respective mortises dry and then gluing and inserting the tenons on one end of each rail into their appropriate mortise. Glue each of the remaining tenons, and slide the other end assembly onto the four exposed tenons. Clamp with bar clamps until the glue has dried. Clean up glue squeeze-out and plane the top of the framework flat.

*Step 16.* Mount the framework to top by boring two pocket holes on one upper rail and screwing the framework to the top. Secure the other half of the top to the frame with some of the available hardware that allows for expansion. Sand, stain and finish with three coats of polyurethane.

# THE LAMPS

I must confess; I don't like much of what passes for lighting in the Arts and Crafts style. The lighting accessories seem to me to anticipate the Art Nouveau movement, which was to replace the Arts and Crafts style. At their worst, most of these lamps are florid and frivolous, and at their best, only adequate. I'm not sure I've done much better here, and with these two lamps, I feel I've strayed as far (or possibly farther) than is permissible under the rigorously enforced style regulations. Nonetheless, I offer these two lamps as Arts and Crafts inspired.

## BUILDING THE LAMPS

*Step 1.* Select wood and match grain patterns.

*Step 2.* Mill wood straight, square and to thickness.

*Step 3.* Glue up panels wide enough for the lamp sides.

*Step 4.* Rip panels to final width.

*Step 5.* Cut ½"-deep groove, ⁵⁄₁₆" wide on center in the 12"-wide panel.

*Step 6.* Rout a dovetail dado, ³⁄₁₆" deep, on center in the 12"-wide panel—the same surface on which you just cut the groove.

*Step 7.* Using the same dovetail bit you used in the previous step, mount the router in horizontal position, and rout a dovetail tenon ³⁄₁₆" deep along the straight, interior edge of one of the 6" sides of the lamp.

**MATERIALS LIST**

### Short Lamp

| NAME | NO. REQ'D | THICKNESS | WIDTH | LENGTH |
|---|---|---|---|---|
| Base Sides | 2 | 1¼" | 12" | 16" |

### Tall Lamp

| NAME | NO. REQ'D | THICKNESS | WIDTH | LENGTH |
|---|---|---|---|---|
| Base Sides | 2 | 1¼" | 12" | 48" |

*Step 8.* Cut the angled cuts of the lamp sides on the band saw.

*Step 9.* Joint these edges.

*Step 10.* Cut the curved interior portions of the 6″ sides on the band saw.

*Step 11.* Cut the curved interior portion of the larger lamp side with a saber saw.

*Step 12.* Sand the interior curves with a drum sander on the drill press.

*Step 13.* Round over the angled edges and the curved portions of the lamp with a ¼″-radius roundover bit mounted in the router.

*Step 14.* Drill ⅛″ holes through the dado and countersink these holes.

*Step 15.* Clamp the smaller lamp side (the one without the dovetail tenon) so that the straight flat edge is up and apply glue.

*Step 16.* Position the larger side in place and drive 1¼″ drywall screws through the drilled and countersunk holes. (The heads of the drywall screws should be completely flush with the bottom of the dado, or the lamp wire will hang up as you're feeding it through the dado.)

*Step 17.* Apply glue to the dado tenon cheeks.

*Step 18.* Slide the dovetailed side in position and allow the glue to dry.

*Step 19.* Bore a ⅜″ hole, 1″ deep at the top of the lamp.

*Step 20.* Epoxy a 2″ piece of threaded pipe into the bored hole.

*Step 21.* Sand the lamp assembly, stain and finish with three coats of polyurethane.

*Step 22.* Thread lamp wire through the interior dado and attach appropriate lamp hardware.

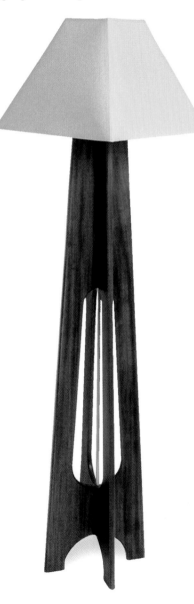

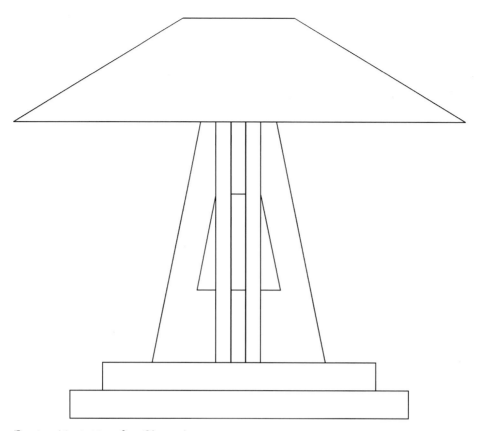

Design Variation for Short Lamp

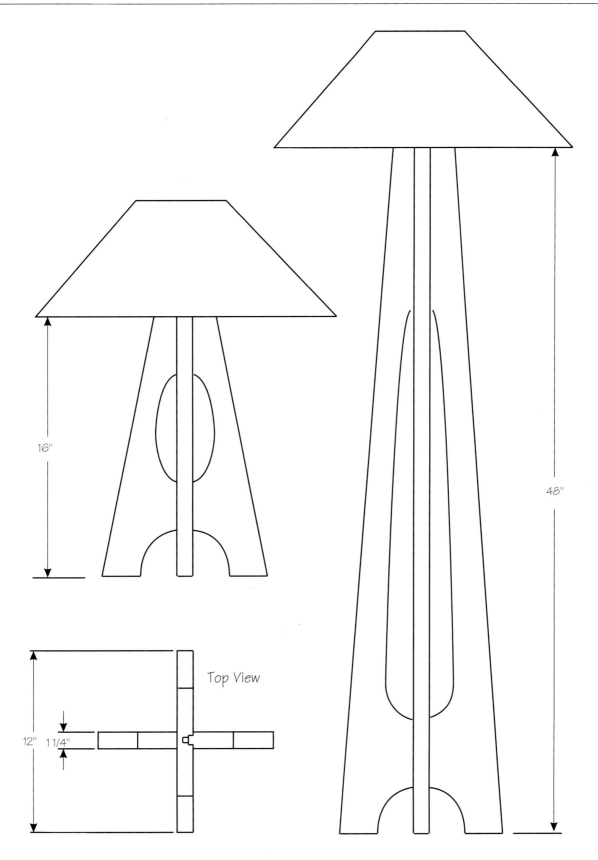

16"

48"

Top View

12"  1 1/4"

# PART THREE

The dining room is perhaps the most diverse room in the home. It serves a function; it's a place to eat and perhaps store china and flatware. But it also serves as a center for family life, whether for entertaining guests or gathering the family. Such a room, by nature, should have furniture that is both useful and beautiful.

"HAVE NOTHING IN YOUR HOUSES
THAT YOU DO NOT KNOW TO BE USEFUL
OR BELIEVE TO BE BEAUTIFUL."

—WILLIAM MORRIS

# THE DINING ROOM

I grew up doing homework at a round dining room table, and that put me at the center of most household activities. Now as I build tables and other dining room accessories for others, I like to think I'm working at something that will still occupy the center of my customer's family, too. With so many difficult forces at work in the American family, this is a notion I cherish.

I build a couple of tables here: a little, round, drop-leaf table and a long, broad, trestle table. There's a serving table, too—a pretty little serving table that carries a slight reminder of that huge sideboard I showed you in the first chaper. And finally, I've built a china cupboard that I've been longing to build since I first saw it.

I mix and match in this chapter. Two of the pieces are à la Stickley and the other two are Greene & Greene inspired. I did this because, first, I wanted to see if the pieces could live together and, second, the customer is always right.

# THE SERVING TABLE

W hen I first began building for a customer's dining room, I aspired to that great big sideboard in chapter one. As I looked at my customer's dining room again and again, that sideboard became smaller and smaller, until finally it ended up a serving table. Generally, my conclusion is that American dining rooms have grown smaller.

The project builds very much like most of the other projects, i.e., through tenons, white oak and beveled edges; but there's a little more scrollwork than most Stickley projects, and there's a large radius curve cut in the back piece of the serving table. Also, you have to rout a shallow groove in the top about 2" from the back so that you can display your china.

## BUILDING THE SERVING TABLE

*Step 1.* Select wood and match grain patterns.

**MATERIALS LIST**

### The Serving Table

| NAME | NO. REQ'D | THICKNESS | WIDTH | LENGTH | NAME | NO. REQ'D | THICKNESS | WIDTH | LENGTH |
|---|---|---|---|---|---|---|---|---|---|
| Side | 2 | ¾" | 18" | 43" | Plate Rail | 1 | ¾" | 1¼" | 38½" |
| Shelf | 2 | ¾" | 16½" | 39¼" | Plate Rail Brackets | 2 | ¾" | 1¼" | 1½" |
| Rail | 4 | ¾" | 1½" | 41" | Drawer Divider Stile | 1 | ¾" | 1" | 6¾" |
| Back | 1 | ¾" | 14" | 39¼" | Drawer Divider | 1 | 1" | 6" | 15⅝" |
| Drawer Front | 2 | ¾" | 6" | 18¾" | Drawer Sides | 4 | ½" | 5" | 15" |
| Foot | 2 | ¾" | 4" | 7¾" | Drawer Back | 2 | ½" | 4½" | 17¼" |
| Lower Drawer Rail | 1 | ¾" | 1½" | 39¼" | Drawer Bottom | 2 | ¼" | 14½" | 17¼" |

*Step 2.* Mill wood square and flat.

*Step 3.* Glue up panels to needed width.

*Step 4.* Mill wood to final dimensions.

*Step 5.* Rout through mortises in sides.

*Step 6.* Rout shallow mortise for bottom front rail.

*Step 7.* Cut through and stub rail tenons to fit mortises.

*Step 8.* Rout mortises for drawer stile in rails.

*Step 9.* Rout stile tenons to fit mortises.

*Step 10.* Rout dadoes for upper and lower shelves.

*Step 11.* Trace pattern on each side.

*Step 12.* Cut scrollwork on each side using band saw or scroll saw, staying 1/16″ from the traced line.

*Step 13.* Clamp the pattern in place and rout the shape on each side using a pattern bit in the router.

*Step 14.* Rout the tongue on the end of each shelf to fit the dado.

*Step 15.* Cut big curve on back.

*Step 16.* Bevel all edges.

*Step 17.* Glue and clamp the rails,

shelves and sides together, checking for squareness.

*Step 18.* Rout rabbets in sides for back.

*Step 19.* Glue and clamp back panel in place.

*Step 20.* Make boxes for drawers.

*Step 21.* Mount drawers.

*Step 22.* Mount drawer fronts.

*Step 23.* Sand and finish with preferred finish.

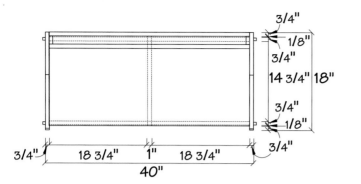

Top View

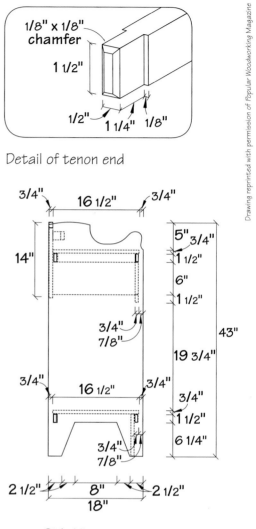

Detail of tenon end

Drawing reprinted with permission of Popular Woodworking Magazine

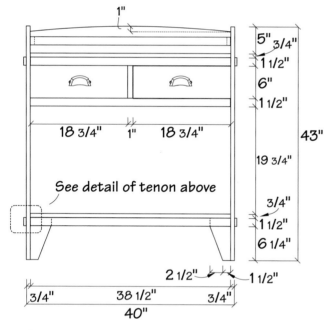

Front View

Side View

# THE CHINA CABINET

Again, this cabinet is a favorite, and it's a project that tests your ability to make light, almost dainty cabinetry. One of the difficulties of the project is dealing with the strips of wood to give that paned look. My friends at *Popular Woodworking* magazine gave me the idea of gluing strips of wood directly to the glass, and that technique seems to work well.

Working with glass is always challenging too, particularly for a guy like me with a "bull in the china shop" phobia. I think that the hardware solution I chose—metal standards and brackets with rubber padding—is the best solution to using glass shelving.

**MATERIALS LIST**

## The China Cabinet

| NAME | NO. REQ'D | THICKNESS | WIDTH | LENGTH |
|---|---|---|---|---|
| Top | 1 | 1" | 18" | 39½" |
| Side Stile | 4 | 1" | 2½" | 66" |
| Side Rail | 4 | 1" | 6" | 13½" |
| Front and Back Stile | 4 | 1" | 6" | 66" |
| Front and Back Rail | 4 | 1" | 6" | 30" |
| Back Center Stile | 2 | 1" | 3" | 62" |
| Bottom Panel | 1 | 1" | 14" | 38" |
| Door Stile | 4 | 1" | 2" | 58¼" |
| Door Rail | 4 | 1" | 2" | 14¾" |
| Back Panel, Plywood | 3 | ¼" | 39½" | 66" |

| HARDWARE | NO. REQ'D | WIDTH | LENGTH | SUPPLIER |
|---|---|---|---|---|
| ¼"-thick Glass Lite | 4 | 9" | 54" | Any hardware store |
| Hinges | 4 | | | Any hardware store |
| Glass Shelf | 4 | 12" | 36" | Any hardware store |

## BUILDING THE CHINA CABINET

*Step 1.* Select wood and match grain patterns.

*Step 2.* Rough-cut parts to size, plus an inch.

*Step 3.* Mill all parts straight and square to thickness and to final size.

*Step 4.* Build front, back and two side assemblies.

*Step 5.* Sand all members through 120-grit sandpaper.

*Step 6.* Make a pattern for cutting the tapered cuts on the face frame stiles.

*Step 7.* Trace pattern on front and back face frame stiles.

*Step 8.* Cut out face frame stiles with a band saw or a saber saw. Cut on the waste side of the pencil line.

*Step 9.* Clamp pattern to each tapered face frame stile and rout it smooth with a pattern bit riding against the pattern's edge.

*Step 10.* Cut slots into the front face frame stiles and rails with a biscuit joiner.

*Step 11.* Insert biscuits, glue and clamp front face frame.

*Step 12.* Cut ¼" groove in the stiles and rails for the door, sides and back for the plywood panels.

*Step 13.* Cut ¼" plywood panel for back.

*Step 14.* Cut stub tenons on rail ends for back and sides.

*Step 15.* Glue tenon stubs; insert into panel groove on the door, back and side stiles. Insert plywood panel and then slide on each mating stile. Clamp and allow to dry.

*Step 16.* Clean up glue squeeze-out, and sand door, sides, back and front face frame.

*Step 17.* Bevel all exposed edges with a beveling bit in a router before carcass assembly.

*Step 18.* Cut biscuit joints in sides, back and front face frame.

*Step 19.* Glue and assemble china cabinet carcass, clamping overnight.

*Step 20.* Glue and screw cleats to lower carcass side rails so that the lower shelf sits flush with the top edge of the bottom rail.

*Step 21.* Build cabinet doors.

*Step 22.* Rout ⅜″ rabbet on three edges of the doors.

*Step 23.* Rout glass rabbet on inside of door frame.

*Step 24.* Fit door to opening; mount door.

*Step 25.* Install glass.

*Step 26.* Cut biscuit slots in cabinet carcass for top installation.

*Step 27.* Screw top to carcass using tabletop hardware in the biscuit slots.

*Step 28.* Sand through 220-grit sandpaper.

*Step 29.* Finish with your preferred wood finish.

Front View

Side View

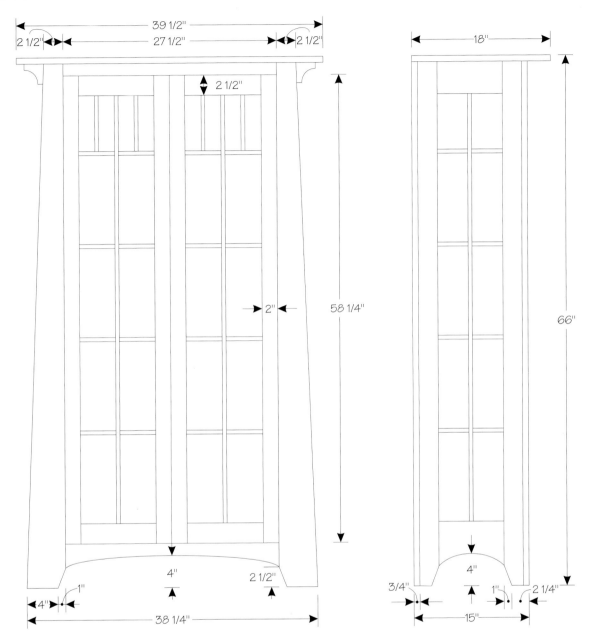

# THE GATELEG BREAKFAST TABLE

T he idea for this table came from Stickley's little gateleg table, the #2820. I've drooled over its elegant lines, its graceful leaves and the sheer utility of a small, round table. The gateleg aspect has always given me pause, however, because those two gatelegs get in the way of chairs around the perimeter, and I demand a table to be more than pretty—I want to be able to use it.

I solved the problem of the gateleg, but it's a hardware solution and some might find this solution less true to the ideals of the Arts and Crafts movement. I disagree, however, as I believe the old craftsmen would have found the judicious use of hardware entirely appropriate.

The solution was part number 29512 from The Woodworkers' Store, a pull-out drop-leaf support. By using this hardware, the footprint of the table's feet measures 24″ square and, even though the table top is 48″ in diameter, the table is extremely solid, even when its leaves are outstretched. The bonus is that you can stick a chair under it anywhere without knocking into the legs or feet. Because of this feature, six people can sit comfortably around this table.

## MATERIALS LIST

### The Gateleg Breakfast Table

| NAME | NO. REQ'D | THICKNESS | WIDTH | LENGTH |
|---|---|---|---|---|
| Top | 1 | 1″ | 48″ | 48″ |
| Leg | 4 | 2½″ | 2½″ | 29″ |
| Side Rail | 4 | 1″ | 3″ | 12½″ |
| Front and Rear Rail | 2 | 1″ | 3″ | 38″ |
| Drop-leaf Pull-out Support | 4 | 1″ | 1½″ | 15″ |
| Lower Rail | 1 | 1″ | 6″ | 38″ |
| Slat | 6 | 1″ | 1½″ | 18″ |

| HARDWARE | NO. REQ'D | PART NO. | SUPPLIER |
|---|---|---|---|
| Drop-leaf Support | 2 pair | 29512 | The Woodworkers' Store |
| Flush Hinge (Drop Leaves) | 2 pair | 28910 | The Woodworkers' Store |

## BUILDING THE GATELEG BREAKFAST TABLE

*Step 1.* Select wood and match grain patterns.

*Step 2.* Mill wood straight, square and to thickness, plus ⅟₁₆″ for final planing.

*Step 3.* Cut foot and leg stock ½″ wider than necessary.

*Step 4.* Rip two ⅜″-thick slices off of the quartersawn faces of the wood and laminate these to the flat-sawn faces so that you have an approximately square leg with quartersawn faces on all four faces.

*Step 5.* Glue up panels wide enough to accommodate the top of the table.

*Step 6.* Surface and sand the panels to final size.

*Step 7.* Rout leaf joint.

*Step 8.* Clamp three pieces of top together.

*Step 9.* Mount router circle cutting jig to underside of the clamped three-piece tabletop unit.

*Step 10.* Cut 48″-diameter top.

*Step 11.* Rout through mortises for front and rear rails.

*Step 12.* Rout stub mortises for upper and lower side rails.

*Step 13.* Rout lower mortise in lower side rails.

*Step 14.* Rout leg mortises in feet.

*Step 15.* Rout slat mortises in upper and lower side rails.

*Step 16.* Cut through, stub and leg tenons with the tenoning jig on the table saw.

*Step 17.* Cut dadoes through upper rails for drop-leaf supports.

*Step 18.* Mount hinges onto tabletop and leaves.

*Step 19.* Glue and assemble side assemblies. (Do not glue slat tenons.)

*Step 20.* Glue front and rear rails and lower shelf tenons.

*Step 21.* Assemble table leg assembly.

*Step 22.* Mount drop-leaf support hardware on the underside of the tabletop.

*Step 23.* Fasten tabletop to leg assembly with top-fastening hardware.

# ❖ GLUING UP LARGE PANELS

The trick to gluing up big panels like this tabletop is establishing a straight, square glue line.

I use an 8′-long piece of plywood that I have painstakingly jointed straight and square as a straightedge. I put a pattern bit in my router and then rout the panel edge straight and square.

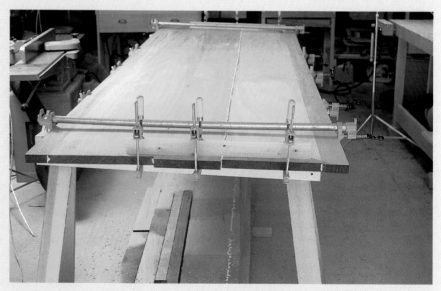

Glue up the panel with biscuit joints every 12″, and draw the assembly together with bar clamps. Use scrap clamped to the tabletop to assure the top is flat.

Top View

Side View

Front View

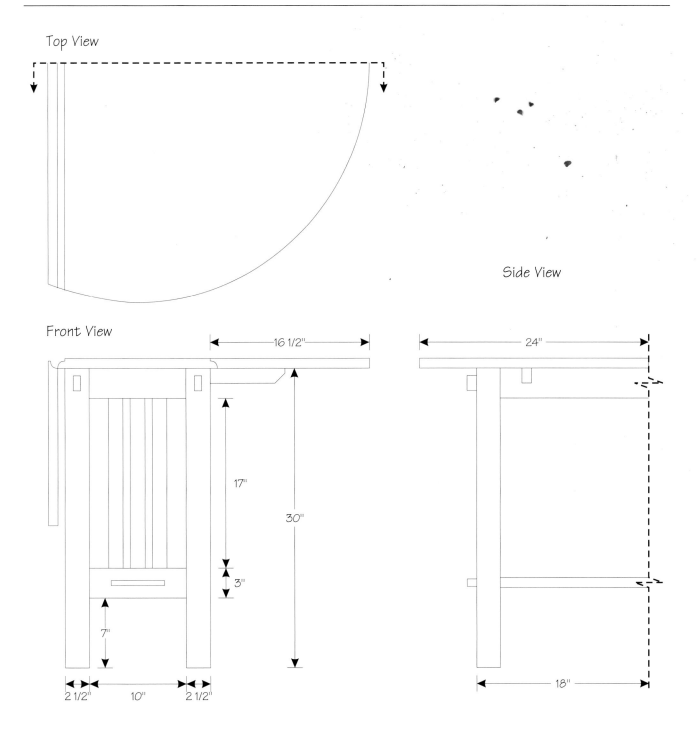

16 1/2"

17"

30"

3"

7"

2 1/2"    10"    2 1/2"

24"

18"

# THE TRESTLE TABLE

I've built lots of tables, but never a trestle table, and certainly never a table as large as this one. I'm not sure why that is, but I'm sure glad this was my first, because I don't know if I could have succeeded early on in my career.

It was challenging for several reasons. First, it's huge—103″ long and 43″ wide. It'll undoubtedly test your ability to build squarely. You can't just pick up a tabletop of this size and blithely joint an edge square. Secondly, once you've got that big top glued up, you can't just run it through your planer, so it's a study in how well you did the first task, getting an edge straight and square, as well as how well you can use a hand plane, scraper or belt sander. Think about each process involved in building something this large, because it takes an extra anticipation of problems. And finally, this table is a challenge to your interpersonal skills because you've got to convince a neighbor or relative to help you tote this big table. Now's the time to cash in those chips from acquaintances who've asked for shelves and help with their Hepplewhite.

## BUILDING THE TRESTLE TABLE

*Step 1.* Have the wood surfaced on all four sides by the seller.

*Step 2.* Examine the wood for the top when you buy the wood.

*Step 3.* Check for cracks, checks, wormholes, etc.

*Step 4.* Check the long planks for flatness and square edges. (Be fussy.)

*Step 5.* When you get home from the wood dealer, match grain patterns and identify which edges belong together.

*Step 6.* Abut the edges that belong together and evaluate the "goodness of fit."

**MATERIALS LIST**

*The Trestle Table*

| NAME | NO. REQ'D | THICKNESS | WIDTH | LENGTH |
|------|-----------|-----------|-------|--------|
| Top | 1 | 1¼″ | 41″ | 104″ |
| Rail | 2 | ¾″ | 6″ | 56″ |
| Crossmember | 2 | 4″ | 6″ | 37″ |
| Leg | 4 | 3″ | 5″ | 18″ |
| Feet | 2 | 4″ | 6″ | 37″ |
| Slats | 10 | 1½″ | 1½″ | 16¾″ |

Top View

104"

41"

*Step 7*. Improve those glueline edges so that they mate perfectly (see "Gluing Up Large Panels" on page 76).

*Step 8*. Use a biscuit joiner to cut biscuit slots about every 12".

*Step 9*. Glue up tabletop into two halves, each approximately 22" wide.

*Step 10*. If you can locate a planer that can plane a top this wide, have the two table halves planed. If you don't have a planer of that capacity, begin hand-planing, scraping and belt-sanding until you have a flat, smooth surface.

*Step 11*. Again, test the glueline between the two table halves.

*Step 12*. Improve the glueline until it is perfect, cut biscuit slots and then glue up the assembly.

*Step 13*. Hand plane, sand and scrape the tabletop flat, smooth and perfect.

*Step 14*. Laminate 8/4 stock to 16/4 for the feet and legs.

*Step 15*. Mill laminated stock and remaining stock to final dimensions.

*Step 16*. Rout leg mortises in the trestle table feet.

*Step 17*. Rout slat mortises in the trestle table feet.

*Step 18*. Rout through mortises in trestle table legs.

*Step 19*. Cut tenons to fit on slats, legs and rails.

*Step 20*. Shape rails and feet to final size and shape.

*Step 21*. Round over feet and leg edges with ¼"-radius roundover bit.

*Step 22*. Bevel slat and rail edges.

*Step 23*. Cut curved ends of tabletop.

*Step 24*. Bevel top edges.

*Step 25*. Assemble table leg assembly.

*Step 26*. Attach top to leg assembly.

*Step 27*. Finish with your preferred kind and color of finish.

Front View

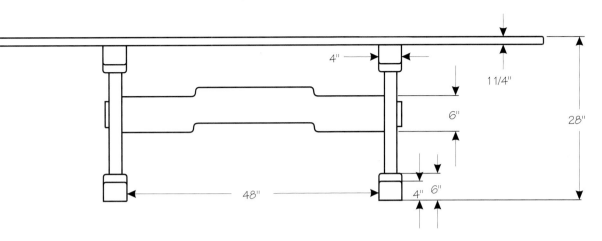

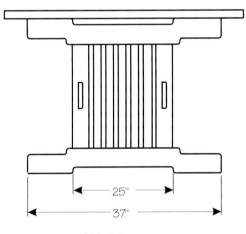

Side View

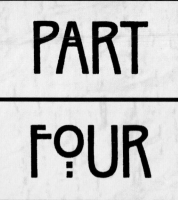

# PART

# FOUR

Comfort and simplicity—the two keys to the ideal bedroom. It must be comfortable to allow the tired worker to sleep soundly. And why should the bedroom afford more than mere pragmatism? Most of the time spent there is in sleep. The rest of the time is in preparation for sleep or for the new day, hence the dresser. But it should also be beautiful, or at least pleasing to the eye, as the bedroom is also a retreat, a solace.

"IN THIS AGE OF AFFECTED ORNAMENTATION, IT IS THE UNIQUE PIECE OF FURNITURE WITH ITS STRIKING, PLEASING OUTLINES AND RIGID SIMPLICITY, AND HARMONIOUS COLORINGS, THAT IS MADE FOR COMFORT AND SERVICE, THAT MARKS THE TASTEFULLY FURNISHED HOME."

—LIMBERT'S ARTS AND CRAFTS FURNITURE CATALOG, CHARLES LIMBERT

# THE BEDROOM

There are few fancy decorations in a Mission-style bedroom and little room for taffeta and lace. In my mind, I see a Navaho blanket or two on the floor or wall, and there are a couple of old family portraits hanging, naturally in quartersawn oak framing. Like the den, there's a masculine feel to the room, and one suspects there might be a shotgun in the closet or at least a pair of well-worn boots.

I built five pieces of furniture for the bedroom: a simple clock, a twin-size bed, a chest of drawers (called a chiffonier in Stickley's catalogs), a little night table called a somnae and a large mirror I've been admiring for a number of years. A couple of the lamps we build in the living room chapter would look good in here, as would the Morris chair; and if we could steal either the tabaret from the den or that round gateleg table from the kitchen, they'd find a happy home right here in the bedroom. For that matter, the secretary would make a nice addition, too, and although I do not build a bookcase in this book, several of the designs for bookcases from Stickley's catalogs would look great.

# THE BEDSTEAD

**MATERIALS LIST**

## The Bedstead

| NAME | NO. REQ'D | THICKNESS | WIDTH | LENGTH |
|---|---|---|---|---|
| Top Headboard Rail | 1 | 1¼″ | 12½″ | 56½″ |
| End Rail | 3 | 1¼″ | 8″ | 56½″ |
| Side Rail | 2 | 1¼″ | 8″ | 75″ |
| Headboard Leg | 2 | 2½″ | 2½″ | 36″ |
| Footboard Leg | 2 | 2½″ | 2½″ | 26¾″ |
| Slat | 20 | 1″ | 1¼″ | 12″ |

| HARDWARE | NO. REQ'D | PART NO. | SUPPLIER |
|---|---|---|---|
| Bed-Rail Fastener | 1 | 28597 | The Woodworkers' Store |
| Center Rail Fastener | 2 | 10025 | The Woodworkers' Store |
| Center Leg (for queen-size only) | 3 | 68429 | The Woodworkers' Store |

Unless this is the first project you build from this book, you are probably already jigged up to cut the mortises for the slats, and you are unerring in cutting through mortises with a router, so I won't bore you with repetitions of earlier work. If you need a refresher, check out page 21 for information on the slat mortising jig and page 20 for how I cut mortise and tenon joints with a router.

What we do need to jaw about, however, is making changes in the basic design to accommodate different mattress sizes. When I began designing this bed, I thought I could stretch it from twin-size all the way through king-size, but I made a full-size mock-up of the king-size bed and it was apparent that I'd never be able to get the proportions right and still carry some semblance of the Mission-style motif. I do believe a queen-size Mission-style bed is possible, with nine slats rather than the five pictured here and bumping up the posts to a full 2½" square.

Another element to consider is whether to use box springs or not. Personally, I find box springs unnecessary, but I like a firm mattress. If you need a set of box springs beneath your mattress, you should lower the rail support system from the dimension shown in the drawing about 5". A set of box springs is typically 7" high. You may want to raise the height of the legs and slats by 2" to make up that 2" difference.

In constructing the bed, I made full use of the most up-to-date hardware I could find, and I urge you to do the same. The bed-rail fasteners allow easy and quick assembly, as do the center rail fasteners. For any bed over twin-size, I like to install a center leg (or three center legs for the queen-size bed) to support the sleepers. Each of these pieces of hardware is available from The Woodworkers' Store (see Sources on page 125).

## BUILDING THE BEDSTEAD

*Step 1.* Select wood and match grain patterns.

*Step 2.* Cut leg stock ½" wider than necessary.

*Step 3.* Rip two ¼"-thick slices off of the quartersawn faces of the wood and laminate these to the flat-sawn faces so that you have an approximately square leg with quartersawn faces on all four faces.

*Step 4.* Mill wood straight, square and to thickness.

*Step 5.* Glue up a panel wide enough for the headboard.

*Step 6.* Surface and sand all members to final thickness.

*Step 7.* Rip and crosscut all parts to final size.

*Step 8.* Cut curves on upper headboard and footboard and sand smooth.

*Step 9.* Mill slat material to size and thickness and sand.

*Step 10.* Rout through leg mortises.

*Step 11.* Chop rounded ends of mortises square with chisel.

*Step 12.* Cut tenons on the table saw with a tenoning jig.

*Step 13.* Fit tenons to mortises.

*Step 14.* Bevel tenon ends.

*Step 15.* Rout slat mortises in the headboard and footboard.

*Step 16.* Cut slat tenons on the table saw with a tenoning jig.

*Step 17.* Chop rounded ends of slat mortises square with chisel.

*Step 18.* Fit slat tenons to mortises.

*Step 19.* Sand all edges and surfaces through 220-grit sandpaper.

*Step 20.* Bevel all exposed edges using a ball-bearing-guided beveling bit in your router.

*Step 21.* Rub in four coats of linseed oil tinted with a dark-fumed oak aniline dye.

*Step 22.* Assemble the two ends of the bed by fitting the slats in place (without glue), and then glue and clamp the four legs in place.

*Step 23.* After the glue has dried, scrape any squeeze-out, sand and repair finish if necessary.

*Step 24.* Cut shallow mortises in the headboard and footboard for the female portion of the rail fastener hardware.

*Step 25.* Chisel out a recess beneath the rail fastener hardware so that the hooks can fully engage the hole of the female portion of the rail fastener hardware.

*Step 26.* Cut shallow mortises in the end grain of each of the side rails for male half of the rail fastener hardware.

*Step 27.* Install the female parts of the two center rail fasteners (three for queen-size beds) ¾″ down from the top edge of each rail (5″ down if you are using box springs), and about one-third of the way down from both ends of each rail.

*Step 28.* Cut two (or three for the queen-size bed) lengths of 2×4 to fit, rail to rail.

*Step 29.* Install the male ends of the center rail fasteners on each end of the 2×4s.

*Step 30.* Install the 2×4s in place.

*Step 31.* Cut two strips of 4/4 scrap long enough to fit on the lower rail of the head- and footboard.

*Step 32.* Drill and countersink ⅛″ holes every 6″ to 8″ on center of these two strips of wood.

*Step 33.* Screw the strips of wood to the inside of the head- and footboard, ¾″ down from the top edge of the rail.

*Step 34.* Cut a piece of ¾″ plywood to fit between the rails, notching the corners to allow for the legs.

## Headboard

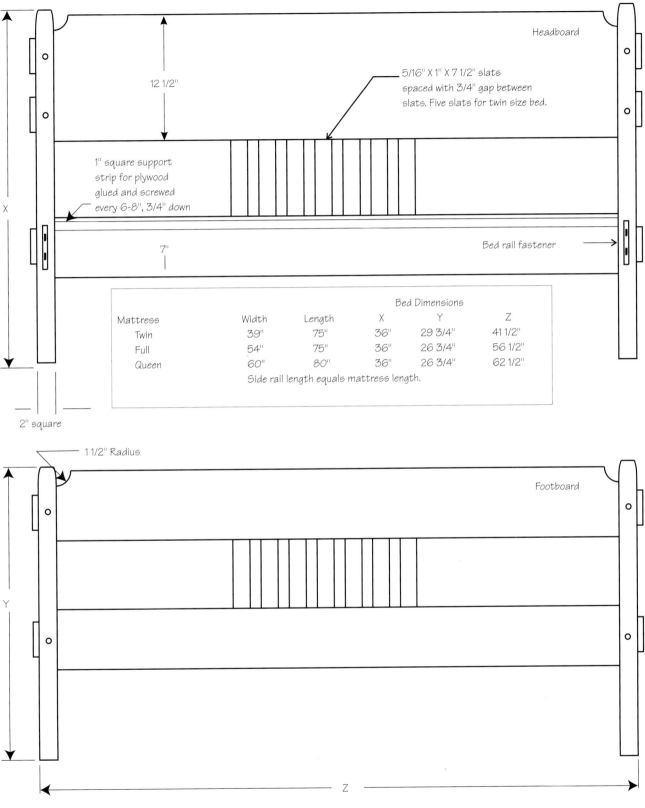

12 1/2"

5/16" X 1" X 7 1/2" slats spaced with 3/4" gap between slats. Five slats for twin size bed.

Headboard

1" square support strip for plywood glued and screwed every 6-8", 3/4" down

Bed rail fastener

X

7"

| Bed Dimensions | | | | | |
|---|---|---|---|---|---|
| Mattress | Width | Length | X | Y | Z |
| Twin | 39" | 75" | 36" | 29 3/4" | 41 1/2" |
| Full | 54" | 75" | 36" | 26 3/4" | 56 1/2" |
| Queen | 60" | 80" | 36" | 26 3/4" | 62 1/2" |

Side rail length equals mattress length.

2" square

1 1/2" Radius

Footboard

Y

Z

## Footboard

Headboard

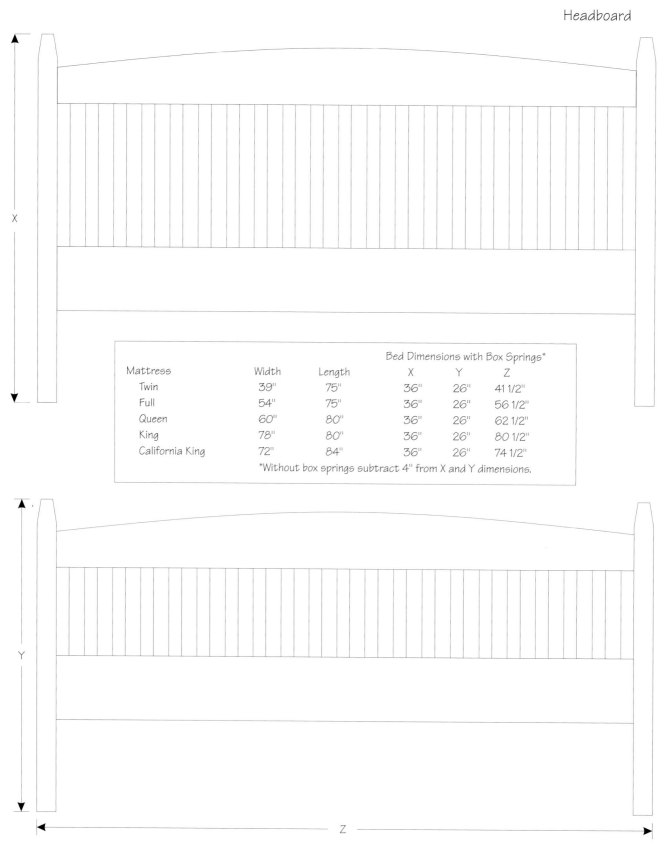

| Mattress | Width | Length | Bed Dimensions with Box Springs* | | |
| --- | --- | --- | --- | --- | --- |
| | | | X | Y | Z |
| Twin | 39" | 75" | 36" | 26" | 41 1/2" |
| Full | 54" | 75" | 36" | 26" | 56 1/2" |
| Queen | 60" | 80" | 36" | 26" | 62 1/2" |
| King | 78" | 80" | 36" | 26" | 80 1/2" |
| California King | 72" | 84" | 36" | 26" | 74 1/2" |

*Without box springs subtract 4" from X and Y dimensions.

Footboard

# THE SOMNAE

When my editor, Adam Blake, first mentioned a somnae, I thought he was talking about a sleep disorder. Luckily, he faxed me a picture of this pretty little night table, and I later had an opportunity to examine one at Craftsman's Farms in Morristown, New Jersey, Stickley's old homestead.

Like several pieces of Stickley's lesser furniture, this piece was built without knowledge of contemporary wood science, for one piece of the carcass was built with no allowance for wood expansion and by rights should have exploded decades ago. It held together, however, no doubt due to some turn-of-the-century magic that we're now unaware of. It's like Tage Frid quipped after Bruce Hoadley published his wood bible, *Understanding Wood*, "Woodworking's got a lot harder since Hoadley invented wood movement."

Anyway, I tried to retain the flavor of that lovely little night table and yet use modern techniques and hardware. You be the judge as to the extent I succeeded.

## BUILDING THE SOMNAE

*Step 1.* Select wood and match grain patterns.

*Step 2.* Rough-cut parts to size plus 1".

*Step 3.* Mill wood straight, square, to thickness and to final size.

**MATERIALS LIST**

## The Somnae

| NAME | NO. REQ'D | THICKNESS | WIDTH | LENGTH |
|---|---|---|---|---|
| Top | 1 | 1″ | 14″ | 19½″ |
| Top Back | 1 | 1″ | 3″ | 19½″ |
| Leg | 4 | 1″ | 3½″ | 30½″ |
| Bottom Rail | 2 | 1″ | 3½″ | 12″ |
| Front Rail | 2 | 1″ | 1″ | 12″ |
| Side Leg | 4 | 1″ | 2½″ | 30½″ |
| Side Rail | 4 | 1″ | 6″ | 7¼″ |
| Door Rail | 4 | 1″ | 1½″ | 15½″ |
| Drawer Side | 2 | ½″ | 4½″ | 10½″ |
| Drawer Front | 2 | ½″ | 4½″ | 11″ |
| Side Panel | 2 | ½″ | 7¾″ | 14½″ |
| Back Panel | 1 | ½″ | 12″ | 23½″ |

| HARDWARE | NO. REQ'D | PART NO. | SUPPLIER |
|---|---|---|---|
| Door Pull | 1 | 123876 | Woodcraft |
| Drawer Pull | 1 | 123875 | Woodcraft |
| Drawer Slide | 1 pair | 27D11 | Woodcraft |

Front View

Side View

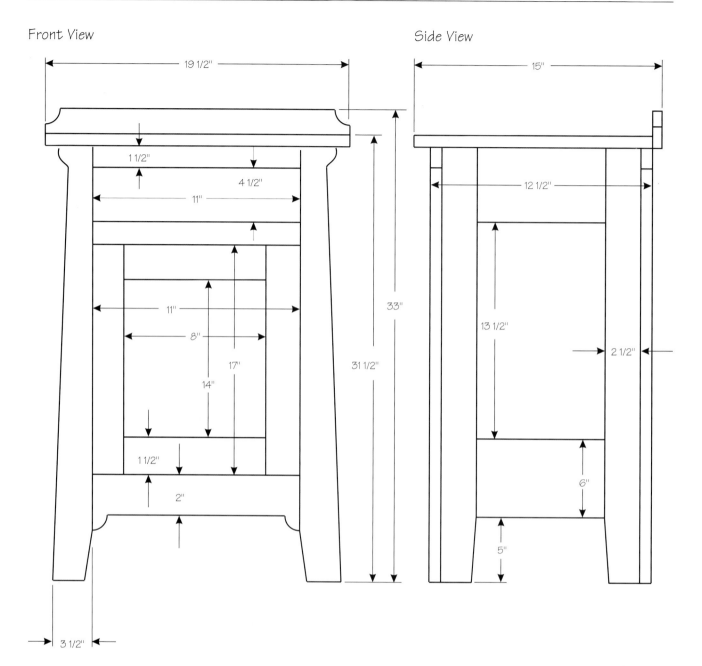

Leg

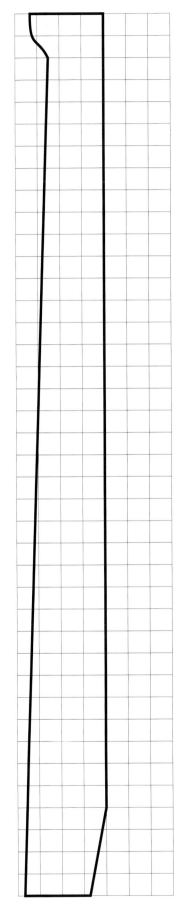

*Step 4.* Glue up a panel wide enough for the top.

*Step 5.* Sand all members through 120-grit sandpaper.

*Step 6.* Make a pattern for cutting the tapered cuts on the face frame stiles as shown in the drawing at left.

*Step 7.* Trace pattern on front and back face frame stiles.

*Step 8.* Cut out face frame stiles with a band saw or a saber saw. Cut on the waste side of the pencil line.

*Step 9.* Clamp pattern to each tapered face frame stile and rout it smooth with a pattern bit riding against the pattern's edge.

*Step 10.* Cut slots into the front face frame stiles and rails with a biscuit joiner.

*Step 11.* Insert biscuits, glue and clamp front face frame.

*Step 12.* Cut ¼" groove in the stiles and rails for the door, sides and back for the plywood panels.

*Step 13.* Cut ¼" white oak plywood panels for the door, back and sides.

*Step 14.* Cut stub tenons on rail ends for back and sides.

*Step 15.* Glue tenon stubs, insert into panel groove on the door, back and side stiles, insert plywood panels and then slide on each mating stile. Clamp and allow to dry.

*Step 16.* Clean up glue squeeze-out and sand door, sides, back and front face frame.

*Step 17.* Bevel all exposed edges before carcass assembly with a beveling bit in a router.

*Step 18.* Cut biscuit joints in sides, back and front face frame.

*Step 19.* Glue and assemble somnae carcass, clamping overnight.

*Step 20.* Glue and screw cleats to lower carcass side rails so that the lower shelf sits flush with the top edge of the bottom rail.

*Step 21.* Rip two blocks of wood to size so that drawer slides mount flush with the sides of the drawer opening.

*Step 22.* Build drawer.

*Step 23.* Mount drawer hardware.

*Step 24.* Install drawer front.

*Step 25.* Fit door to opening and mount door.

*Step 26.* Install drawer and door pulls.

*Step 27.* Cut biscuit slots in cabinet carcass for top installation.

*Step 28.* Screw top to carcass using tabletop hardware in the biscuit slots.

*Step 29.* Sand through 220-grit sandpaper.

*Step 30.* Finish with two coats of boiled linseed oil colored with dark-fumed oak aniline dye.

# THE CHIFFONIER

Occasionally, you build something that really turns out nice, and every time you see it or open one of its drawers you get a rush of pleasure that's almost sinful. That's the feeling I get every time I use this chest of drawers.

I suspect Stickley had an affinity for chests because he built a whole bundle of variations on this theme, almost all more complex than this one I've chosen to build. Some have little cabinets up top in lieu of those two smaller drawers, and I've seen a couple of wardrobes with drawers on the inside, as well as room for hanging clothes. To my eye, each one is a masterpiece of function and proportion.

Avoiding the expansion problems of solid wood panels, I've chosen to use white oak plywood panels in the sides and back. I wish I could find quartersawn white oak plywood, but I have only very occasionally run across such a thing.

## BUILDING THE CHIFFONIER

*Step 1.* Select wood and match grain patterns.

*Step 2.* Cut leg stock ½″ wider than necessary.

*Step 3.* Rip two ⅛″-thick slices off of the quartersawn faces of the wood and laminate these to the flat-sawn faces so that you have an approximately square leg with quartersawn faces on all four faces.

*Step 4.* Mill all other wood straight, square and to thickness.

*Step 5.* Rout through mortises in the legs.

*Step 6.* Chop mortises square with mortising chisel.

*Step 7.* Rip a ¼″ groove for the side panels on center in each of the legs.

*Step 8.* Rip a ¼″ groove for the back panels on center in each of the back legs.

*Step 9.* Cut stile tenons for the carcass sides and the back stiles on the table saw using the tenoning jig.

*Step 10.* Rip a ¼″ groove on center in each of the stiles, stopping the groove before the tenon exits the mortise.

*Step 11.* Bevel all exposed edges with a beveling bit in the router before assembly.

*Step 12.* Glue up stile tenons, insert into the corresponding mortise, insert the plywood panel and then slide the other leg onto the remaining tenons.

*Step 13.* Clamp overnight.

*Step 14.* Clean up glue; sand through 180-grit sandpaper.

*Step 15.* Lay out location of drawer stiles on the inner surface of the front legs.

*Step 16.* Bore five ½″ holes, ½″ deep with a Forstner bit.

*Step 17.* Chop these holes into ¼″-square mortises with chisels.

Front View

Side View

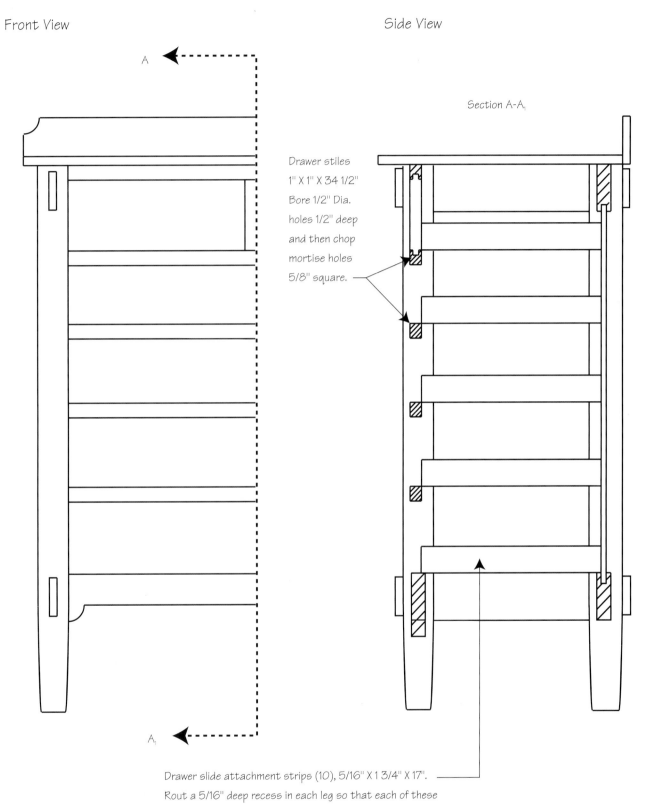

A

Section A-A₁

Drawer stiles
1" X 1" X 34 1/2"
Bore 1/2" Dia.
holes 1/2" deep
and then chop
mortise holes
5/8" square.

A₁

Drawer slide attachment strips (10), 5/16" X 1 3/4" X 17".
Rout a 5/16" deep recess in each leg so that each of these
strips lies flush with the inside surface of the leg.

*Step 18.* Rout a ½″ mortise for the lower stile, ⅝″ deep into the inner surfaces of the front legs.

*Step 19.* Bore two ½″ holes, ½″ deep into the two upper drawer stiles for the divider between the two upper drawers.

*Step 20.* Chop these holes into ⅝″-square mortises.

*Step 21.* Cut the ⅝″-square tenons on the stile ends and the divider ends using the tenoning jig on the table saw.

*Step 22.* Rout the ⁵⁄₁₆″-deep × 1¾″-wide × ⅜″-long recess for the drawer slide attachment strips.

*Step 23.* Chop the recesses square or round the corners of the drawer slide attachment strips.

*Step 24.* Glue and screw the drawer slide attachment strips in place.

*Step 25.* Glue up the stub tenons on the divider and slip them into the mortises on the two upper drawer stiles.

*Step 26.* Bore a couple of ⅛″ holes through the upper two drawer stiles and into the divider, countersink and then drive two 1¼″ drywall screws into the divider.

*Step 27.* Saw the stub tenons on the lower drawer stile to fit the mortises in the legs using the tenoning jig on the table saw.

*Step 28.* Band saw the curved shape of the lower drawer stile.

*Step 29.* Sand shaped portion of the lower drawer stile smooth.

*Step 30.* Glue up the tenons on each of the drawer stiles, including the tenons on the lower drawer stile and the back stiles.

*Step 31.* Insert the glued tenons of all of the stiles into the mortises on one side.

*Step 32.* Slide the back plywood panel in place.

*Step 33.* Position the other side atop the tenon ends and clamp the carcass assembly with bar clamps, checking for square.

## MATERIALS LIST

### The Chiffonier

| NAME | NO. REQ'D | THICKNESS | WIDTH | LENGTH |
|------|-----------|-----------|-------|--------|
| Leg | 4 | 1¾″ | 1¾″ | 47″ |
| Top | 1 | 1″ | 21¼″ | 42″ |
| Front Rail | 5 | 1″ | 1″ | 34½″ |
| Side Rail | 4 | 1″ | 5″ | 20″ |
| Lower Front Rail | 1 | 1″ | 3½″ | 34½″ |
| Back Rail | 2 | 1″ | 3″ | 34½″ |
| Short Drawer Front and Back | 4 | 1″ | 6½″ | 16¼″ |
| Short Drawer Bottom | 2 | ¼″ | 17¼″ | 16¼″ |
| Short Drawer Sides | 4 | ½″ | 6½″ | 17¼″ |
| Long Drawer Sides | 8 | ½″ | 6½″ | 17¼″ |
| Long Drawer Front and Back | 8 | ½″ | 6½″ | 33½″ |
| Long Drawer Bottom | 4 | ¼″ | 17¼″ | 33″ |
| Back | 1 | ¼″ | 34″ | 38″ |

| HARDWARE | NO. REQ'D | PART NO. | SUPPLIER |
|----------|-----------|----------|----------|
| Large Drawer Pull | 8 | 123874 | Woodcraft |
| Small Drawer Pull | 2 | 123875 | Woodcraft |
| Drawer Slide | 6 | 01V07 | Woodcraft |

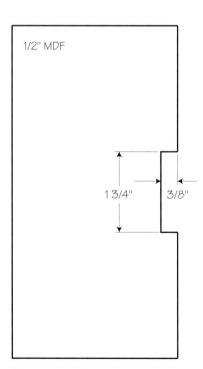

Drawer Slide Support Strip
Recess Routing Pattern

Sectional View

Side View

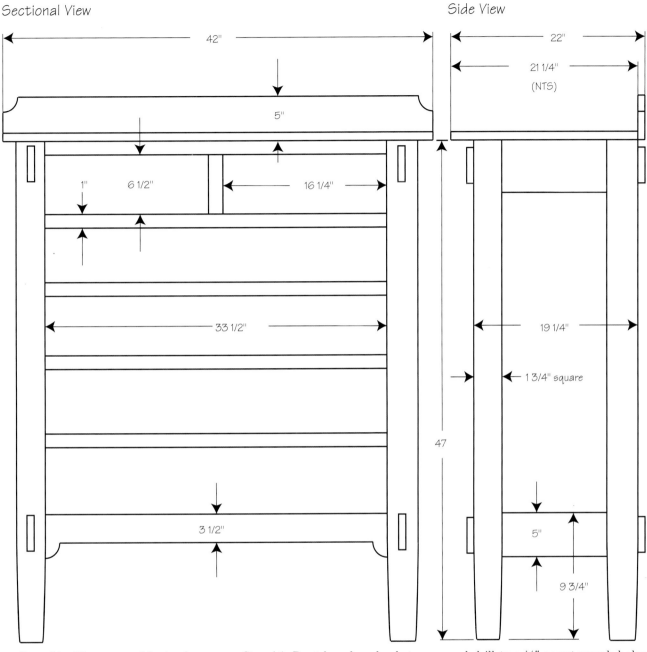

**Step 34.** Allow assembly to dry, then clean up squeeze-out.

**Step 35.** Build drawer boxes.

**Step 36.** Cut drawer fronts to fit the drawer openings.

**Step 37.** Install drawer slides.

**Step 38.** Mount drawer fronts on drawer boxes.

**Step 39.** Install drawer pulls.

**Step 40.** Cut the top backstop to size and shape.

**Step 41.** Rout bevel on backstop and top with a beveling bit.

**Step 42.** Glue and screw backstop to back edge of the chest top.

**Step 43.** Screw two no. 10 round head wood screws into the end grain of each back leg.

**Step 44.** Rout keyhole slots to fit the two screwheads on the underside of the chest top.

**Step 45.** Slide top into position

and drill two ⅛″ countersunk holes through the upper front rail.

**Step 46.** Screw two 1¼″ drywall screws into the underside of the chest top.

**Step 47.** Sand through 220-grit sandpaper.

**Step 48.** Finish with two coats of boiled linseed oil colored with dark-fumed oak aniline dye.

# THE MIRROR

In a similar fashion to the clock, this mirror does much to foster the feel of authenticity or completion in a Mission-style room. In the same fashion that I urge you to buy the best wood, buy the best mirror, too. Don't opt for the ⅛"-thick stuff that might get you by; shell out the extra cash for the ¼" plate mirror and have them bevel the edges with 1½" bevel all around the perimeter of the mirror. It makes a big difference in how the end product turns out.

There's more than one way to hang the mirror. The more decorative method is to locate the studs in the wall where you want to hang the mirror and then drive two 2" no. 10 round head wood screws into the studs. Use a level to make sure the screws are exactly at the same height. Next mark the centerline of the screws onto the upper stile of the mirror with a pencil. On the backside of the upper stile, draw two lines down from those marks. Use a keyhole router bit to rout two recesses that the heads of the wood screws fit into.

**MATERIALS LIST**

*The Mirror*

| NAME | NO. REQ'D | THICKNESS | WIDTH | LENGTH |
|---|---|---|---|---|
| Vertical Rail | 2 | 1¼" | 4" | 30" |
| Horizontal Rail | 2 | 1¼" | 4" | 45" |

| HARDWARE | NO. REQ'D | PART NO. | SUPPLIER | |
|---|---|---|---|---|
| Glass Retainer Pads (pkg of 10) | 6 | 28530 | The Woodworkers' Store | |

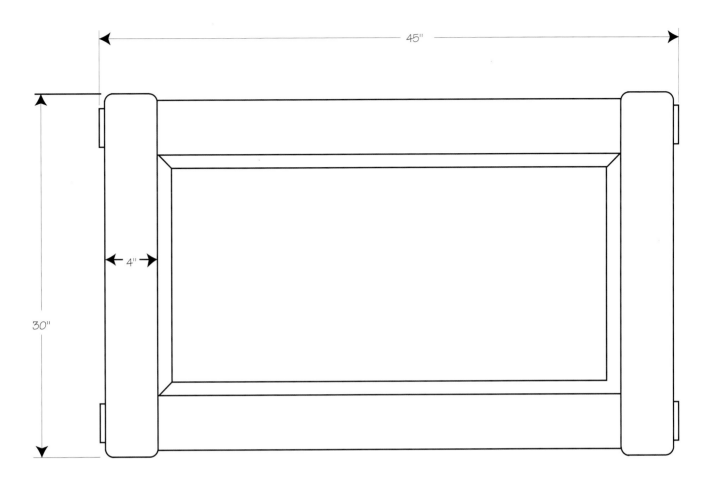

## BUILDING THE MIRROR

*Step 1.* Select wood and match grain patterns.

*Step 2.* Mill wood to size and thickness.

*Step 3.* Begin to cut slip mortise on the table saw with the tenoning jig.

*Step 4.* Finish the cut on the table saw using the rip fence as a guide to continue the cut begun with the tenoning jig.

*Step 5.* Hand-saw out the remainder of the saw-kerf, then chop out the waste with a mortising chisel.

*Step 6.* In the same fashion, begin cutting the tenon to size with the tenoning jig, making tentative ad-

justments on a piece of scrap until you get a good fit for the mortises, and then completing the saw-kerfs by running the workpieces on edge into the sawblade and using the rip fence as a guide. I like to clamp a stop block to the rip fence and behind the sawblade so that I don't cut too far.

*Step 7.* Remove waste by installing a dado head on the table saw and crosscutting until the tenon is complete.

*Step 8.* Glue up the mirror frame and clamp until dry. Glue and insert appropriately sized white oak spacers the same thickness as the tenons into the gap at the top of each mor-

tise and clamp these in place.

*Step 9.* Trim spacers to size, clean up glue squeeze-out and sand the mirror frame through 180-grit sandpaper. Finish with two coats of boiled linseed oil colored with dark-fumed oak aniline dye.

*Step 10.* Rout beveled edges on all exposed edges.

*Step 11.* Rout a rabbet around the back interior perimeter of the mirror frame for the mirror to fit into.

*Step 12.* Rout recesses for the tapered pads that hold the mirror in place.

*Step 13.* Insert mirror and screw tapered pads in place.

*Step 14.* Mount mirror.

# THE CLOCK

After years of trying to get a room to look authentic in one style or another, I've finally decided that it's the accessories that actually carry much of the unnoticed ambiance of a room—a picture, a rug or perhaps this little clock. There's no way I can claim this as an authentic Mission-style piece, although I've seen similar pieces put forth as such.

It is, of course, essentially a board with a hole in it to house one of those ubiquitous battery-powered clock mechanisms that you find in all of the woodworking catalogs. I have tinkered quite a bit with the dimensions of this little clock, and although I'm not entirely satisfied with it, I do feel it's getting there. You might want to experiment with the dimensions, angles and proportions to fine-tune this clock for your mantelpiece.

## BUILDING THE CLOCK

*Step 1.* Select wood and match grain patterns.

*Step 2.* Mill wood to size and thickness.

*Step 3.* Crosscut clock body to final angled shape with miter gauge on table saw.

*Step 4.* Rip angled faces on base and top. I used my tenoning jig for the end cuts.

*Step 5.* Cut a 3″ circle through a piece of ½″ medium density fiberboard (MDF).

*Step 6.* Clamp the MDF circle pattern and rout a round recess in the clock body for the clock mechanism, using a plunge router with a template guide mounted on the baseplate to rough out the opening. Follow with a fixed-base router fitted with a pattern bit to rout to final diameter and depth.

*Step 7.* Drill two ⅛″ holes through the top and base pieces and countersink the holes.

*Step 8.* Attach top and base pieces to the clock body with 1¼″ drywall screws.

*Step 9.* Laminate a piece of 1/16″-thick white oak to the top to hide the screw holes.

*Step 10.* Sand through 220-grit sandpaper.

*Step 11.* Finish with two coats of boiled linseed oil colored with dark-fumed oak aniline dye.

*Step 12.* Insert clock mechanism.

Front View

Side View

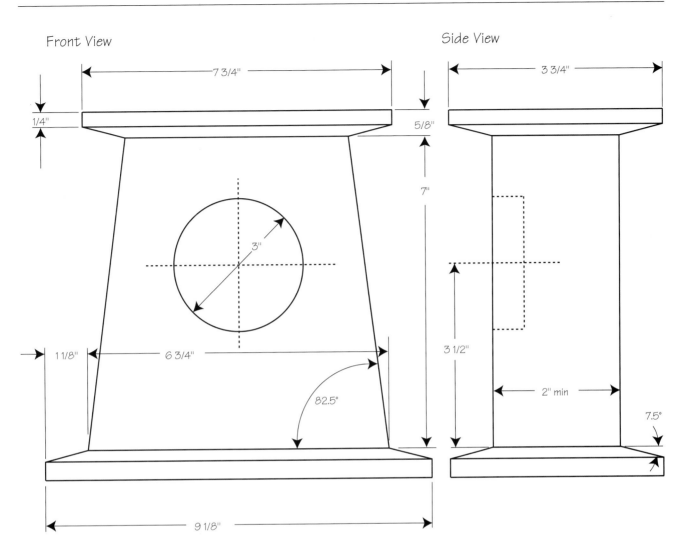

7 3/4"

1/4"

5/8"

3 3/4"

7"

3"

1 1/8"

6 3/4"

82.5°

3 1/2"

2" min

7.5°

9 1/8"

MATERIALS LIST

## The Clock

| NAME | NO. REQ'D | THICKNESS | WIDTH | LENGTH |
|------|-----------|-----------|-------|--------|
| Clock Body | 1 | 2" | 6¾" | 7" |
| Top | 1 | ⅝" | 3¾" | 7¾" |
| Base | 1 | ⅝" | 3¾" | 9⅛" |

| HARDWARE | PART NO. | SUPPLIER |
|----------|----------|----------|
| Battery-Powered Clock Mechanism | 24068 | The Woodworkers' Store |

# PART FIVE

We work all day, and then we come home. It's the effort of our working—whether at a job, on our houses or on our relationships—that keeps it all together. The den is a place to get away from it all; its very name evokes images of refuge. Again, it will take a little effort to create that place of refuge. Whether it's used as a place to relax with a cup of coffee or a place to sit down and take care of the bills, the den and its surroundings add to the comfort of our homes.

"BY HAMMER AND HAND
DO ALL THINGS STAND."

—FROM A HAMMERED COPPER FIREPLACE HOOD
AT GUSTAV STICKLEY'S CRAFTSMAN FARMS

# CHAPTER FIVE

# THE DEN

My family and I visited Yellowstone National Park last summer. There's lots of Arts and Crafts furniture in the Mammoth Hot Springs Hotel and the Old Faithful Lodge. We spotted a number of Stickley chairs that had been in everyday use in the dining room at Old Faithful Lodge for over 80 years—now that's the kind of furniture that belongs in a den.

When I think of a den, I see books, a billiard table and hunting and fishing gear. Even though its currently shunned, there's a faint odor of tobacco in the room, as if cigars are welcome, and there's probably a snifter or two of brandy in one of the cubbyholes. There's no TV or kids within, but dogs are welcome. It's a very masculine room—in my mind at least—filled with the hearty kinds of masculine comforts that men enjoy.

There's probably no better room for Arts-and-Crafts-style furniture. The heavy, honest substance of these five pieces of furniture invites use. It's clear these are not "foo-foo" show pieces; we have everyday work expectations for them. Like those Stickley chairs, they are expected to bear their burdens for countless generations.

# THE SECRETARY

This magnificent little writing desk is perfect for a single-purpose pursuit—for example, fly-tying, writing, storing genealogical records or even just doing the monthly bills. If you can't have a room of your own, at least you can have your own desk. There's a bookshelf on top for storing all of the reference books pertaining to your specialty, and inside are lots of slots and cubbyholes for organizing and storing your stuff. Best of all, the desk is only 13″ wide and 48″ tall—you can fit it practically anywhere.

This desk is a fine example of the Arts and Crafts style and uses most of the stylistic motifs found in Arts and Crafts furniture. I have used dovetailing in the cabinet carcass and in the drawer construction, but the project is amenable to simpler joinery if you prefer. I used simpler joinery on the interior cabinetry using single-kerf dadoes to locate and secure the corresponding tongues on the interior crosspieces.

## BUILDING THE SECRETARY

*Step 1.* Select wood and match grain patterns.

*Step 2.* Mill wood straight, square and to thickness, plus ⅟₁₆″ for final planing.

*Step 3.* Cut leg stock ½″ wider than necessary.

*Step 4.* Rip two ⅛″-thick slices off of the quartersawn faces of the wood

and laminate these to the flat-sawn faces so that you have an approximately square leg with quartersawn faces on all four faces.

*Step 5.* Glue up panels wide enough to accommodate the sides, top and bottom of the cabinet and the top of the table.

*Step 6.* Surface and sand the panels to final size.

*Step 7.* Make a pattern as shown in the drawing on page 110.

*Step 8.* Trace the pattern on the sides of the cabinet and saw it out. Remember to stay proud of the line in the waste portion of the cut.

*Step 9.* Now clamp the pattern in place and rout the edge smooth with a pattern bit.

*Step 10.* Rout two mortises in each side.

*Step 11.* Cut end tenons to width by holding the board perpendicular to the table saw while running it against the rip fence.

*Step 12.* Cut end tenons to length on the table saw sled by holding the board perpendicular to the sled and firmly against the sled's fence.

*Step 13.* Cut dovetails in cabinet sides using a Keller dovetail jig.

*Step 14.* Rip upper shelf to size and at angle, and bevel all exposed edges with a beveling bit in the router.

*Step 15.* Assemble cabinet.

*Step 16.* Trim dovetails with belt sander.

*Step 17.* Cut rabbet in back of cabinet for ¼″ plywood back.

*Step 18.* Make bevel cuts on feet

with the radial arm saw, table saw or chop saw.

*Step 19.* Cut mortises in feet and square them up with a chisel.

*Step 20.* Cut tenons on ends of legs with tenoning jig on the table saw.

*Step 21.* Cut through mortises on the back legs with the router.

*Step 22.* Cut through mortises on the front legs with the router.

*Step 23.* Cut two mortises 1″ deep on the back legs with the router.

*Step 24.* Square up the round mortises with a chisel.

*Step 25.* Bore a ⅝″-diameter hole into the side of the front legs ½″ deep with a Forstner bit on the drill press.

*Step 26.* Square up the round holes to ⅝″ square.

*Step 27.* Cut tenons with the tenoning jig on the table saw.

*Step 28.* Fit tenons to mortises, sand, finish and then assemble the table assembly.

*Step 29.* Fit drawer front to opening.

*Step 30.* Build drawer.

*Step 31.* Mount drawer hardware; install drawer.

*Step 32.* Mount drawer pulls; attach front to drawer.

*Step 33.* Bore four ⅛″ holes through top and into each leg.

*Step 34.* Countersink and screw 2″ drywall screws into each hole.

*Step 35.* Fit folding secretary front to opening.

*Step 36.* Mount hinges onto front and mark where the shelf hits the front.

## MATERIALS LIST

### The Secretary

| NAME | NO. REQ'D | THICKNESS | WIDTH | LENGTH |
|---|---|---|---|---|
| Cabinet Front | 1 | 1″ | 28½″ | 21″ |
| Cabinet Back | 1 | ¼″ | 16½″ | 29″ |
| Cabinet Side | 2 | 1″ | 13″ | 21″ |
| Leg | 4 | 3″ | 3″ | 26″ |
| Foot | 2 | 3″ | 3″ | 15″ |
| Upper Back | 1 | 1″ | 5″ | 29½″ |
| Cabinet Bottom | 1 | 1″ | 15¼″ | 32½″ |
| False Drawer Front | 1 | 1″ | 4″ | 25½″ |
| Drawer Front and Back | 2 | ¾″ | 4″ | 25½″ |
| Drawer Side | 2 | ¾″ | 4″ | 12″ |
| Drawer Bottom | 1 | ¼″ | 12″ | 25″ |
| Side Rail | 2 | 1″ | 5″ | 7″ |
| Front Rail | 1 | 1″ | 1″ | 26½″ |
| Shelf | 1 | 1″ | 9″ | 29½″ |
| Divider | 8 | ½″ | 6″ | 6″ |
| Divider Side | 2 | ½″ | 12″ | 15″ |
| Crosspiece | 2 | ½″ | 9¾″ | 28″ |
| Upright | 2 | ½″ | 12″ | 9½″ |
| Drawer Box Bottom | 2 | ½″ | 12″ | 6″ |
| Middle | 1 | ½″ | 3″ | 16″ |
| Door | 2 | ½″ | 6½″ | 6½″ |
| Bottom Rail | 1 | 1″ | 5″ | 32½″ |
| Small Drawer Front and Back | 4 | ½″ | 2½″ | 5½″ |
| Small Drawer Side | 4 | ½″ | 2½″ | 9″ |
| Small Drawer Bottom | 2 | ¼″ | 5½″ | 9″ |

Front View

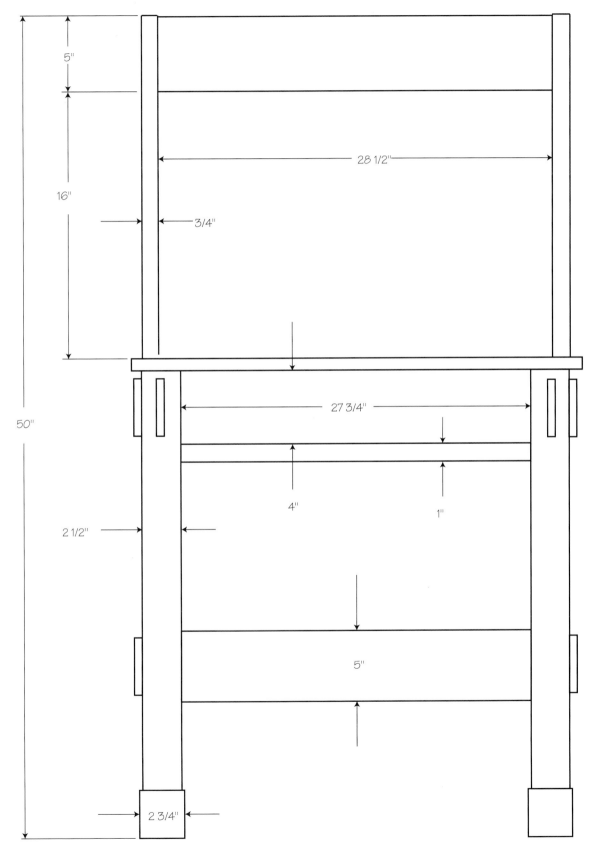

5"

28 1/2"

16"

3/4"

50"

27 3/4"

4"

1"

2 1/2"

5"

2 3/4"

*Step 37.* Trim secretary front to size and angle.

*Step 38.* Build the two interior cabinet frames.

*Step 39.* Make little boxes.

*Step 40.* Cut cabinet doors to size.

*Step 41.* Mount cabinet doors.

*Step 42.* Build middle divider.

*Step 43.* Dismantle and sand all edges and surfaces through 220-grit sandpaper.

*Step 44.* Bevel all exposed edges using a ball-bearing-guided beveling bit in your router.

*Step 45.* Rub in four coats of linseed oil tinted with a dark-fumed oak aniline dye.

*Step 46.* Insert and clamp the two interior boxes and the middle partition in place.

*Step 47.* Drill pilot holes and countersink 1″ drywall screws in inconspicuous places to position and hold the interior components in place.

*Step 48.* Glue and nail the ¼″ plywood backing in place.

*Step 49.* Screw on the back to the bookshelf area now.

Side View

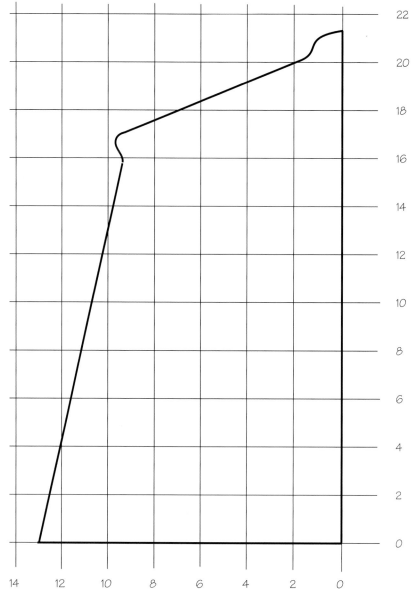

Inside View

Full Side View

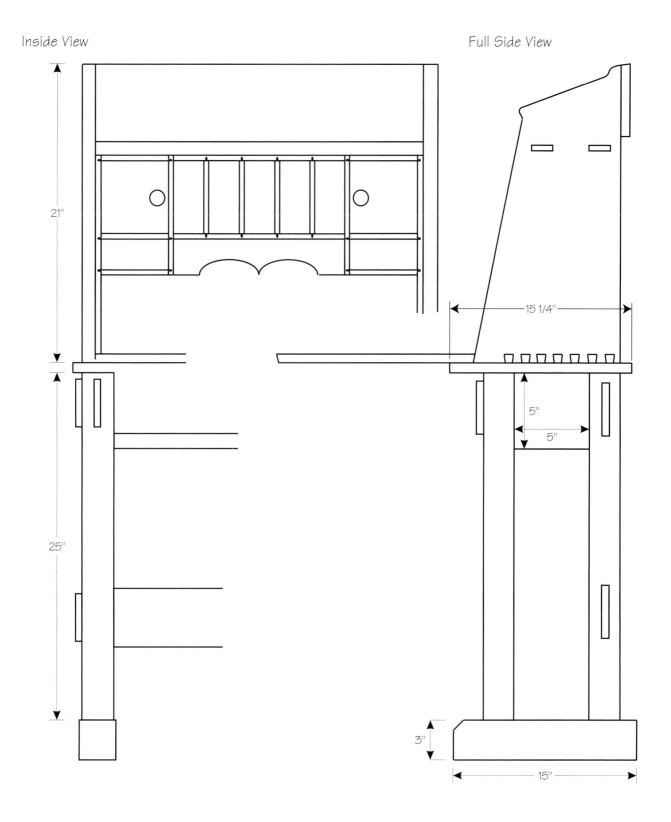

21"

25"

15 1/4"

5"

5"

3"

15"

# THE COFFEE TABLE

I love this little table. It's gorgeous, solid as a battleship and easy to build. You have to use nearly all of the characteristic Arts and Crafts techniques, and with its broadly overhung top, it reminds me rather of Frank Lloyd Wright's "Falling Water" home.

Now anyone who knows Mission-style furniture also knows it's a study in mortise and tenon joinery, and as I sketched out the plans to build a couple of Mission-style coffee tables, I was suddenly faced with cutting 80 mortises and 80 tenons—far too many for delicate lilies such as myself, and I'm certain even the burly, ham-fisted woodworkers of yore wilted before such tasks. But, given the impetus of a couple of paying customers, it didn't take me long to figure out a way to

**MATERIALS LIST**

## The Coffee Table

| NAME | NO. REQ'D | THICKNESS | WIDTH | LENGTH |
|---|---|---|---|---|
| Top | 1 | 1¼″ | 24¾″ | 48″ |
| Slat | 16 | ⅜″ | 1½″ | 8″ |
| Leg | 4 | 2½″ | 2½″ | 16½″ |
| Side Rail | 4 | 1″ | 2½″ | 44″ |
| End Rail | 4 | 1″ | 2½″ | 16″ |

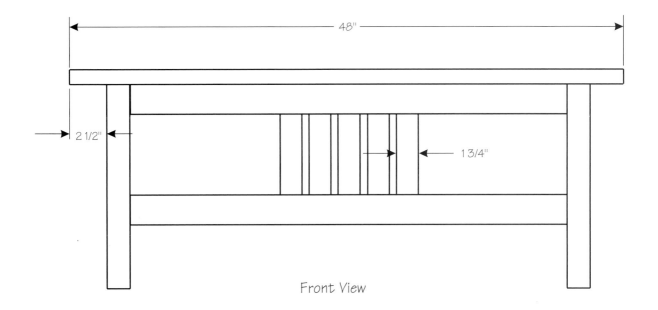

48"

2 1/2"

1 3/4"

Front View

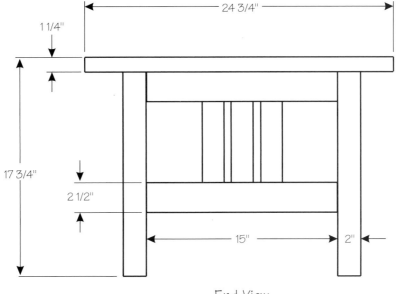

24 3/4"

1 1/4"

17 3/4"

2 1/2"

15"

2"

End View

rout mortises safely, accurately and, most importantly, fast. You'll find information about routing shallow mortises for slats and the jig I developed in chapter one on page 21.

## BUILDING THE COFFEE TABLE

*Step 1.* Select wood and match grain patterns.

*Step 2.* Cut leg stock ½" wider than necessary.

*Step 3.* Rip two ⅛"-thick slices off of the quartersawn faces of the wood and laminate these to the flat-sawn faces so that you have an approximately square leg with quartersawn faces on all four faces.

*Step 4.* Mill wood straight, square and to thickness.

*Step 5.* Glue up panels wide enough for the top.

*Step 6.* Surface and sand the top to final thickness.

*Step 7.* Rip and crosscut the top to final size.

*Step 8.* Mill rail and slat material to size and thickness and sand.

*Step 9.* Rout through leg mortises.

*Step 10.* Rout side mortises 1" deep.

*Step 11.* Chop rounded ends of mortises square with chisel.

*Step 12.* Cut tenons on the table saw with a tenoning jig.

*Step 13.* Fit tenons to mortises.

*Step 14.* Bevel tenon ends.

*Step 15.* Rout slat mortises.

*Step 16.* Cut slat tenons on the table saw with a tenoning jig.

*Step 17.* Chop rounded ends of slat mortises square with chisel.

*Step 18.* Fit slat tenons to mortises.

*Step 19.* Sand all edges and surfaces through 220-grit sandpaper.

*Step 20.* Bevel all exposed edges using a ball-bearing-guided beveling bit in your router.

*Step 21.* Rub in four coats of linseed oil tinted with a dark-fumed oak aniline dye.

*Step 22.* Assemble the two coffee table ends by fitting the slats in place (without glue) and then gluing and clamping the four end rails in place.

*Step 23.* After the glue has dried, scrape any squeeze-out, and sand and repair finish, if necessary.

*Step 24.* Assemble the coffee table frame by inserting the slats into each of their respective mortises dry and then gluing and inserting the tenons on one end of each rail into their appropriate mortise.

*Step 25.* Glue each of the remaining tenons and slide the other end assembly onto the four exposed tenons.

*Step 26.* Clamp with bar clamps until the glue has dried.

*Step 27.* Clean up glue squeeze-out, plane the top of the framework flat and sand and repair the finish, if necessary.

*Step 28.* Mount framework to top by boring two pocket holes on one upper rail and screwing the framework to the top.

*Step 29.* Secure the other half of the top to the frame with some of the available hardware that allows for expansion.

# THE TABARET

I love this little table. For me, it's what Plato was talking about in his *Allegory of the Caves*, when he said, "There really is only one table, that icon or shape we see when we close our eyes and imagine a table." This is the table I see; which is not to say you cannot modify its design. I've built it taller and with a smaller top than many, to suit the den, but you could easily enlarge the top to as much as 40″ in diameter and lower the height of the top to as much as 26″ to serve as a small dining or work table. I've also seen this table with a bentwood apron stretching from leg to leg that looks quite handsome, but I prefer the ease of construction found in this table. Cutting the mortises at an angle was rather a challenge, but I've included some tips within step-by-step instructions.

## BUILDING THE TABARET

*Step 1.* Select wood and match grain patterns.

*Step 2.* Mill wood straight, square and to thickness, plus ¹⁄₁₆″ for final planing.

*Step 3.* Cut leg stock ½″ wider than necessary.

*Step 4.* Rip a ⅛″-thick slice off of one of the quartersawn faces of the wood for the legs, and laminate this to what will be the outer flat-sawn faces so that you have a rectangular-shaped leg with quartersawn faces on three faces.

**MATERIALS LIST**

### *The Tabaret*

| NAME | NO. REQ'D | THICKNESS | WIDTH | LENGTH |
|---|---|---|---|---|
| Top Board | 4 | 1¼″ | 8″ | 32″ |
| Leg | 4 | 2″ | 2″ | 28½″ |
| Brace | 2 | 1″ | 3″ | 28″ |
| Crosspiece | 2 | 1¼″ | 2¾″ | 28″ |

CLASSIC ARTS & CRAFTS FURNITURE YOU CAN BUILD

*Step 5.* Glue up the top.

*Step 6.* Surface and sand all materials to final size.

*Step 7.* Cut cylindrical top to size.

*Step 8.* Sand edge of cylindrical top.

*Step 9.* Cut top and bottom of legs to size and at 7° angle.

*Step 10.* Cut brace dadoes.

*Step 11.* Rout 1"-deep mortises in braces.

*Step 12.* Square mortises with chisel.

*Step 13.* Cut tenon cheeks on tenoning jig on table saw.

*Step 14.* Cut the perpendicular cheeks on angled face of the leg by clamping angled upper end of leg in position on table saw sled. Use stop block.

*Step 15.* Cut bottom leg mortises as per photos on page 20.

*Step 16.* Taper legs to an exact square at the bottom of the leg using a tapering jig on the table saw.

*Step 17.* Assemble legs in upper braces.

*Step 18.* Drill and countersink screw holes through the brace mortises and into the legs.

*Step 19.* Screw in four 2" drywall screws.

*Step 20.* Position lower cross-brace across legs and clamp in place.

*Step 21.* Mark along both sides of each leg to show where the tenon enters and emerges from the mortise.

*Step 22.* Saw tenons on tenoning jig and finish saw cut by hand if saw blade doesn't reach high enough.

*Step 23.* Crosscut tenons to length using the miter gauge set at 83° and 97° angles for each side of the brace.

*Step 24.* Fit the tenon to the mortise.

*Step 25.* Trim tenon to final length.

*Step 26.* Sand all edges and surfaces through 220-grit sandpaper.

*Step 27.* Bevel all exposed edges using a ball-bearing-guided beveling bit in your router.

*Step 28.* Rub in four coats of linseed oil tinted with a dark-fumed oak aniline dye.

*Step 29.* Assemble.

Top View

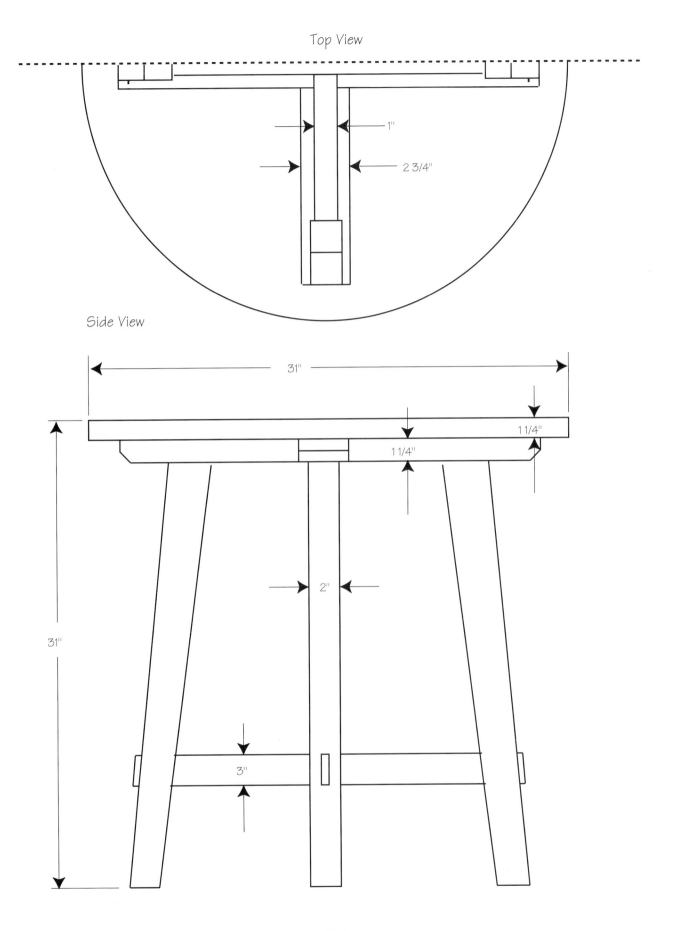

Side View

# THE HALL TREE

I t's not home until you have a place to hang your hat," Stickley should have said. He didn't; I did. There are lots of exemplars of coat trees or hall trees in the literature of the times, and I've seen a bunch of different renditions. How far can you stretch a base and a pole? Well, to muddy the waters further, I thought I'd try my own version of an Arts and Crafts hall tree with kind of a Frank Lloyd Wright look to it.

This is as simple a project as can be. The only tricky part is getting the rays displayed on all four sides of the pole. As talked about in chapter one, for many pieces of furniture, Stickley used a lock-miter joint on four pieces of quartersawn 4/4 white oak and therefore glued up a square beam with the rays displayed on all four sides. Obviously, I couldn't use a hollow beam for this project, so I just ripped ⅛″ slices off the quartersawn faces and laminated them to the flat-sawn sides.

## BUILDING THE HALL TREE

*Step 1.* Select wood and match grain patterns.

*Step 2.* Rip two ⅛″-thick slices off of the quartersawn faces of the tree.

*Step 3.* Laminate the ⅛″-thick slices to the flat-sawn faces so that you end up with an approximately square beam with quartersawn faces on all four faces.

*Step 4.* Mill all wood straight, square and to thickness.

*Step 5.* Surface and sand all pieces to final size.

*Step 6.* Trim the coat tree top bevel to size on the radial arm saw or with a chop saw.

*Step 7.* Lay the coat tree across two base pieces.

*Step 8.* Center one end of the tree on a base piece by measuring from both ends of the base piece with a combination square.

*Step 9.* When the tree is exactly centered, draw lines on the base piece to show the innermost limits of the dadoes.

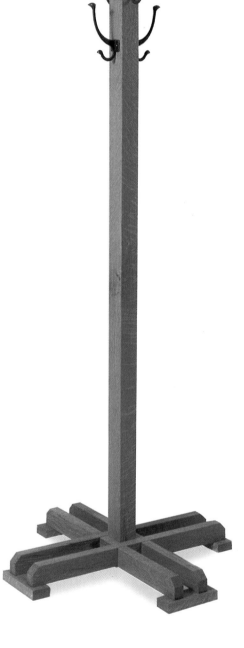

## MATERIALS LIST

### The Hall Tree

| NAME | NO. REQ'D | THICKNESS | WIDTH | LENGTH |
|---|---|---|---|---|
| Tree | 1 | 2½″ | 2½″ | 75″ |
| Base | 4 | 1¼″ | 2″ | 26″ |
| Pad | 4 | 1″ | 2½″ | 6″ |

| HARDWARE | | | |
|---|---|---|---|
| NAME | NO. REQ'D | PART NO. | SUPPLIER |
| 1¼″ Drywall Screws | 12 | | Any hardware store |
| Coat Hooks | 4 | 123877 | Woodcraft |

*Step 10.* Use the miter gauge to carry two of the base pieces squarely across the ¾″ dado head and the rip fence to position the base.

*Step 11.* Cut the remainder of the 1¼″-wide dado ¼″ deep on both sides of two of the base pieces by moving the fence slightly to the right.

*Step 12.* Measure the exact halfway point of one of the ¼″-deep dadoes, and raise the dado head to cut that deep.

*Step 13.* Now cut four ¾″-wide dadoes on center with the 1¼″-wide dado from the *bottom* of the two base pieces. Use the rip fence as a guide for these cuts.

*Step 14.* Using the same rip fence settings as a guide, use the miter gauge to cut a ¾″-wide dado from the *top* of the other two base pieces.

*Step 15.* Saw a 45° bevel on all eight upper ends of the base pieces.

*Step 16.* Sand all edges and surfaces through 220-grit sandpaper.

*Step 17.* Bevel all exposed edges using a ball-bearing-guided beveling bit in your router.

*Step 18.* Rub in four coats of linseed oil tinted with a dark-fumed oak aniline dye.

*Step 19.* Drill and countersink four ⅛″ holes through the midpoint of the base pieces.

*Step 20.* Assemble the base pieces and slide the tree into position.

*Step 21.* Screw four 1⅝″ drywall screws through the base pieces and into the tree.

*Step 22.* Mount the four footpads in position by drilling, countersinking and screwing eight drywall screws into the base pieces.

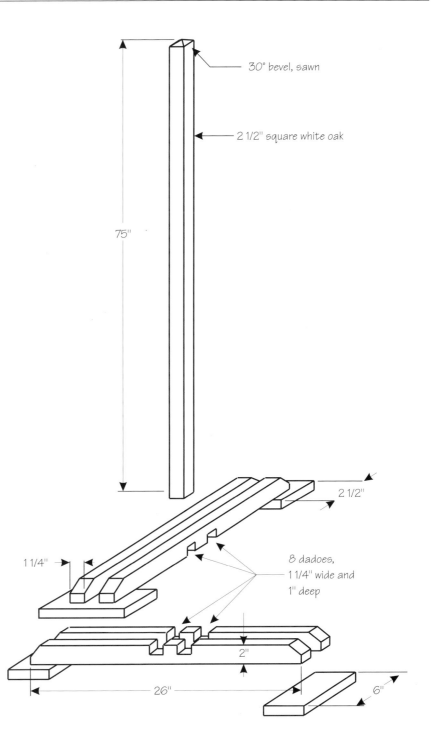

30° bevel, sawn

2 1/2″ square white oak

75″

2 1/2″

1 1/4″

8 dadoes,
1 1/4″ wide and
1″ deep

2″

26″

6″

# THE PEDESTAL

Among the accessories that every home needs in multiples are pedestals. They're perfect for displaying art, for setting globes upon or for showing off bouquets of flowers. You can even set your spouse upon one, should he/she be so worthy.

With some pieces of furniture, it's difficult to find a historic example that carries all of the style characteristics. This is true of this pedestal. Only the beveled-edge work, the rectilinear top, the fumed oak stain and the thick quartersawn white oak retain the sense that this is an Arts and Crafts piece.

Because this pedestal is largely curvilinear, it requires me to show techniques for sawing and shaping perfect identical curves. This piece doesn't use mortise and tenon joinery either, so I've shown how I cut the sliding dado joint here, too. Look for instructions on how to do both in the step-by-step instructions.

## BUILDING THE PEDESTAL

*Step 1.* Select wood and match grain patterns.

*Step 2.* Mill wood straight, square and to thickness, plus ¹⁄₁₆″ for final planing.

*Step 3.* Glue up panels wide enough to accommodate the two interlocking base pieces and top.

*Step 4.* Surface and sand the panels to final size.

**MATERIALS LIST**

### The Pedestal

| NAME | NO. REQ'D | THICKNESS | WIDTH | LENGTH |
|---|---|---|---|---|
| Base Pieces | 2 | 1¼″ | 14″ | 36½″ |
| Top | 1 | 1¼″ | 14″ | 14″ |

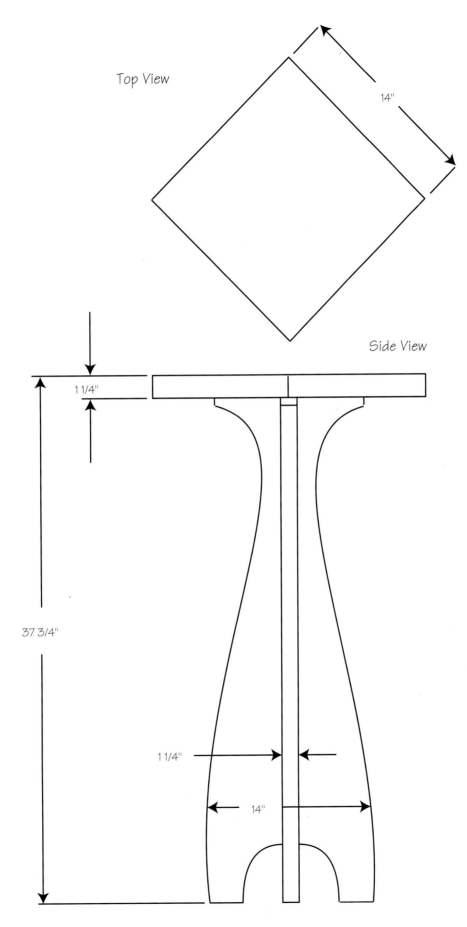

Top View

14"

Side View

1 1/4"

37 3/4"

1 1/4"

14"

*Step 5.* Cut the pattern shape at right onto a piece of ½"-thick MDF or void-free plywood.

*Step 6.* Sand the pattern's edges smooth and square.

*Step 7.* Cut a 1¼"-wide dado ¼" deep on center on both sides of one base piece, using a ¾"-wide dado head mounted on the table saw.

*Step 8.* Measure the exact halfway point, top to bottom, of the two base pieces, and draw a square line on both sides of each of the base pieces.

*Step 9.* Cut a ¾"-wide dado through, on center, from the *bottom* to the *middle* of that same base piece on which you cut the 1¼"-wide dado.

*Step 10.* Cut a ¾"-wide dado through, on center, from *top* to the *middle* of the other base piece.

*Step 11.* Chisel a square end to each of the ¾" dadoes at the midpoint of each of the base pieces.

*Step 12.* Slip a piece of scrap ¾" wood into the dado, slide the pattern in position against the scrap and trace the pattern shape onto each side of the base piece blanks.

*Step 13.* Cut out pattern shape on each side of the base piece blanks.

*Step 14.* Cut out the base piece shape on the band saw or with a saber saw. (Stay within ¹⁄₁₆" on the waste side of the line.)

*Step 15.* Reinsert the ¾" scrap into the ¾" dado, reposition the pattern in place, and clamp.

*Step 16.* Rout the pattern's shape on all four edges of the base pieces with a ½"-diameter pattern bit 1"

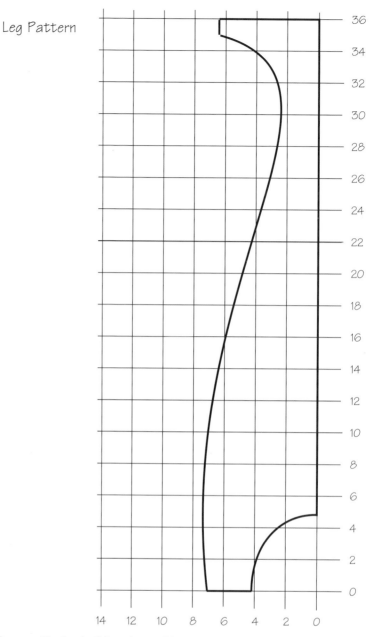

Leg Pattern

long, with the ball bearing guide riding along the MDF pattern. You will need to make a second pass with the pattern bit after you've removed the pattern, to cut the full 1¼" width of the base piece.

*Step 17.* Cut the top square and to size.

*Step 18.* Sand all edges and surfaces through 220-grit sandpaper.

*Step 19.* Bevel all exposed edges using a ball-bearing-guided beveling

bit in your router.

*Step 20.* Rub in four coats of linseed oil tinted with a dark-fumed oak aniline dye.

*Step 21.* Drill two holes through the wings of one base piece and countersink those holes for a 1⅝"-long drywall screw.

*Step 22.* Slide the two base pieces together, turn it upside down atop the bottom of the top, and screw in two 1⅝"-long drywall screws.

## Dadoed Blanks

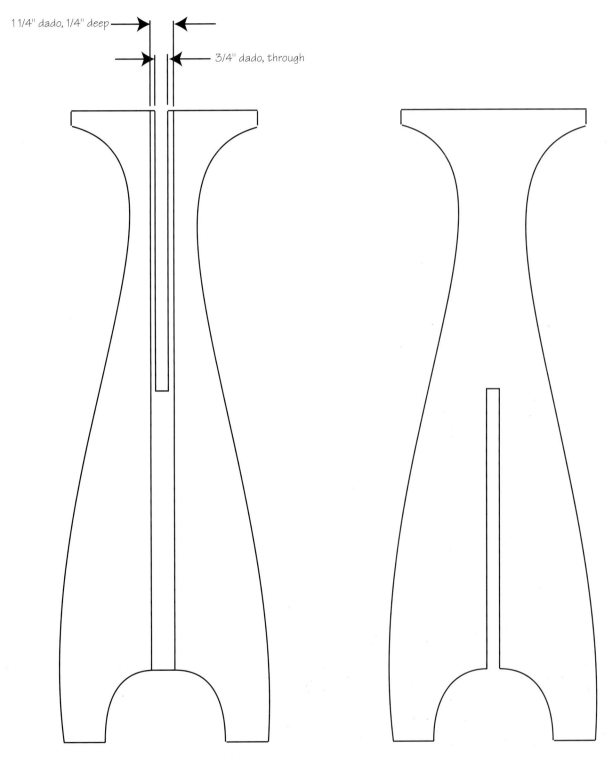

1 1/4" dado, 1/4" deep

3/4" dado, through

# ❖ SOURCES OF SUPPLY

**GENERAL WOODWORKING SUPPLIERS**

Garrett Wade
161 Avenue of the Americas
New York, NY 10013
(800) 221-2942

Highland Hardware
1045 N. Highland Avenue NE
Atlanta, GA 30306
(800) 241-6748

The Woodworkers' Store
4365 Willow Drive
Medina, MN 55340
(800) 279-4441

Trendlines
135 American Legion Highway
Revere, MA 02151
(800) 767-9999

William Alden
27 Stuart Street
Boston, MA 02116
(800) 249-8665

Woodcraft Supply Corp.
210 Wood County Industrial Park
P.O. Box 1686
Parkersburg, WV 26102-1686
(800) 225-1153

Woodworker's Supply, Inc.
1108 North Glenn Road
Casper, WY 82601
(800) 645-9292

**HARDWARE SUPPLIERS**

Woodworker's Hardware
P.O. Box 180
Sauk Rapids, MN 56379
(800) 383-0130

**ROUTER SUPPLIERS**

CMT Tools
310 Mears Boulevard
Oldsmar, FL 34677
(800) 531-5559

Eagle America
P.O. Box 1099
Chardon, OH 44024
(800) 872-2511

Woodhaven
5323 W. Kimberly
Davenport, IA 52806
(800) 344-6657

**WOOD SUPPLIERS**

Bristol Valley Hardwoods
4054 Bristol Valley Road
Bristol, NY 14424
(800) 724-0132

Hardwood Heaven
1620 S. 3rd Street
Lincoln, NE 68501
(402) 477-5989

Steve Wall Lumber Co.
544 River Road
P.O. Box 287
Mayodan, NC 27027

# ❖ ADDITIONAL ARTS AND CRAFTS REFERENCES

Copeland, P.A., and J.H. Copeland, eds. *1912 Quaint Furniture Catalog*. Parchment, Mich.: Parchment Press, 1993.

Dresdner, M. *The Woodfinishing Book*. Newtown, Conn.: The Taunton Press, 1992.

Duginske, M. *Mastering Woodworking Machines*. Newtown, Conn.: The Taunton Press, 1992.

Gray, Stephen, *Quaint Furniture in Arts and Crafts*. New York: Turn of the Century Editions, 1988.

Makinson, Randell L. *Greene & Greene: Furniture and Related Designs*. Layton, Utah: Gibbs Smith, 1997.

Mayer, Barbara. *In the Arts & Crafts Style*. San Francisco: Chronicle Books, 1993.

Windsor, H.H., ed. *Mission Furniture: How to Make It (Parts I, II and III, Complete)*. New York, Dover Publications, 1980.

# ❖ INDEX

# More Great Books for Your Woodshop!

**Creating Beautiful Boxes With Inlay Techniques**—Now building elegant boxes is easy with this handy reference featuring 13 full-color, step-by-step projects! Thorough directions and precise drawings will have you creating beautiful inlaid boxes with features ranging from handcut dovetails to hidden compartments. #70368/$24.99/128 pages/230 color, 30 b&w illus./paperback

**The Woodworking Handbook**—Spend more time working with wood and less time shuffling through pages! This landmark reference is packed with the woodworking specifics you need to know—on topics from adhesives, design, finishing and safety to sharpening, supplies, tools and workshop math. #70371/$21.99/224 pages/199 b&w illus.

**Build Your Own Kitchen Cabinets**—Build beautiful, sturdy kitchen cabinets, no matter what your skill level! Step-by-step directions walk you through planning, design, construction and installation. And a range of cabinetry designs will ensure that the cabinets you build are the right ones for you! #70376/$22.99/136 pages/170+ b&w illus./paperback

**Mastering Hand Tool Techniques**—Get the most from your hand tools! Over 180 tools are detailed with step-by-step instructions on how to use and care for them properly. Plus, you'll make the most of your work with tips on wood selection, precise measuring and flawless sawing, turning, carving and joinery. #70364/$27.99/144 pages/300+ color illus.

**Earn a Second Income From Your Woodworking**—Turn your hobby into income with the stories of 15 professional woodworkers and the secrets they used to make their dream come true! You'll get the inside story on business planning, marketing, workshop design and tax issues to help you make the most of your dreams, too! #70377/$22.99/128 pages/42 b&w illus./paperback

**Build Your Own Router Tables**—Increase your router's accuracy, versatility and usefulness with a winning table design. Detailed plans and instructions for 3 types of tables plus a variety of specialty jigs and fixtures will help you create the right table for your shop. #70367/$21.99/160 pages/300 b&w illus./paperback

**The Encyclopedia of Joint Making**—Create the best joints for every project! This comprehensive resource shows you how to prepare lumber, prevent layout errors, select the right joint, choose the best fastener and more. #70356/$22.99/144 pages/300+ color illus.

**The Woodworker's Guide to Furniture Design**—Discover what it takes to design visually pleasing and comfortably functional furniture. Garth Graves shows you how to blend aesthetics and function with construction methods and material characteristics to develop designs that really work! #70355/$27.99/208 pages/110 b&w illus.

**Build Your Own Entertainment Centers**—Now you can customize the construction and design of an entertainment center to fit your skill level, tools, style and budget. With this heavily illustrated guidebook, you'll explore the whole process—from selecting the wood to hardware and finishing. #70354/$22.99/128 pages/229 b&w illus./paperback

**Good Wood Finishes**—Take the mystery out of one of woodworking's most feared tasks! With detailed instructions and illustrations you'll learn about applying the perfect finish, preparing materials, repairing aged finishes, graining wood and much more. #70343/$19.99/128 pages/325+ color illus.

**Measure Twice, Cut Once, Revised Edition**—Miscalculation will be a thing of the past when you learn these effective techniques for checking and adjusting measuring tools, laying out complex measurements, fixing mistakes, making templates and much more! #70330/$22.99/144 pages/144 color illus./paperback

**100 Keys to Woodshop Safety**—Make your shop safer than ever with this manual designed to help you avoid potential pitfalls. Tips and illustrations demonstrate the basics of safe shopwork—from using electricity safely and avoiding trouble with hand and power tools to ridding your shop of dangerous debris and handling finishing materials. #70333/$17.99/64 pages/125 color illus.

**Making Elegant Gifts From Wood**—Develop your woodworking skills and make over 30 gift-quality projects at the same time! You'll find everything you're looking to create in your gifts—variety, timeless styles, pleasing proportions and imaginative designs that call for the best woods. Plus, technique sidebars and hardware installation tips make your job even easier. #70331/$24.99/128 pages/30 color, 120 b&w illus.

**Getting the Very Best From Your Router**—Get to know your router inside and out as you discover new jigs and fixtures to amplify its capabilities, as well as techniques to make it the most precise cutting tool in your shop. Plus, tips for comparing different routers and bits will help you buy smart for a solid long-term investment. #70328/$22.99/144 pages/225+ b&w illus./paperback

**Good Wood Handbook, 2nd Edition**—Now you can select and use the right wood for the job—before you buy. You'll discover valuable information on a wide selection of commercial softwoods and hardwoods—from common uses, color and grain to how the wood glues and takes finish. #70329/$19.99/128 pages/250 color illus.

**100 Keys to Preventing and Fixing Woodworking Mistakes**—Stop mistakes before they happen—and fix those that already have. Numbered tips and color illustrations show you how to work around flaws in wood; fix mistakes made with the saw, plane, router and lathe; repair badly made joints, veneering mishaps and finishing blunders; assemble projects successfully and more! #70332/$17.99/64 pages/125 color illus.

**How to Sharpen Every Blade in Your Woodshop**—You know that tools perform best when razor sharp—yet you avoid the dreaded chore. This ingenious guide brings you plans for jigs and devices that make sharpening any blade short and simple! Includes jigs for sharpening boring tools, router bits and more! #70250/$17.99/144 pages/157 b&w illus./paperback

**The Woodworker's Source Book, 2nd Edition**—Shop for woodworking supplies from home! Charles Self has compiled listings for everything from books and videos to plans and associations. Each listing has an address and telephone number and is rated in terms of quality and price. #70281/$19.99/160 pages/50 illus.

---